Sex Differences in Personality: Readings

edited by

Dirk L. Schaeffer
The University of Alberta

Brooks / Cole Publishing Company
Belmont, California
A Division of Wadsworth Publishing Company, Inc.

L. C. Cat. Card No.: 76-139686
Printed in the United States of America

1 2 3 4 5 6 7 8 9 10—75 74 73 72 71

Preface

Although more research effort in personality constructs has been devoted to the identification of sex differences than to any other single dimension, this research, and the theories associated with it, has seldom been presented in any summary form. This book attempts both to bring together a series of significant articles on research and theory in this area and to provide a loose structure for their integration.

To achieve these goals, I have been forced to make several arbitrary decisions, not only with regard to the individual selections but also with regard to the criteria for their selection and the framework within which they are set. For example, I have not included any studies dealing with sex differences in intelligence, school achievement, and the like. The mass of such studies is overwhelming, and they are, I feel, of only tangential interest to the subject of personality. I have also given far less emphasis to developmental studies than their number would warrant, primarily because most of the work in this area is so excellently summarized in Eleanor Maccoby's *Development of Sex Differences*. Furthermore, I have adopted the approach of trying to classify most selections in terms of their relevance to either Freudian or social learning theories of development. Although these distinctions are highly artificial, they provided the opportunity for relating the selections to one another and for setting them into a common conceptual framework.

Finally, I have arbitrarily divided the book into three sections —again primarily for ease of presentation of the material rather than because I feel strongly that it is the *only* way to divide the area. The first section, Perception of the Self and Others, deals with the way people of both sexes feel about themselves and others in terms of often unconscious attitudes, expectations, and prejudices. The second section, Intrapersonal and Interpersonal Behavior, discusses some of the behavioral manifestations of sex differences that research has discovered. I have attempted here to avoid the obvious, assuming that most of us know, for example, that girls are more likely than boys to play with dolls. Instead, I have tried to find areas (such as dreaming, vocational values, and controlled play activities) in which the differences are not so obvious. The final section, Sex-Related Behavior, deals with sex differences in the psychological expression of sexuality. It examines the effects of sex role and of some differences in physiological sexual functions (within normal limits) on sex-related behaviors.

Each section, as well as each selection, is prefaced by a sometimes brief, sometimes lengthy introduction to the given topic. I hope, thereby, to have provided enough background and fill-in material to give the reader a fairly comprehensive picture of the area, as well as some challenging examples of the research that can be conducted.

The book took an unconscionable amount of time to put together. Much of that time was devoted to the agonizing task of making decisions, any of which could have been unfair to somebody and most of which probably were. David Lynn, Jaques Kaswan, Hershel Thornburg, Leona Tyler, Gerald Blum, and P. James Geiwitz read large portions of the book and offered insightful and practical comments on it. Generally, the harsher their opinion, the more useful it turned out to be; but all of them made getting kicked a pleasure. Lew Goldberg, in several conversations, helped clarify a number of problem areas for me and let me kick back. The people at Brooks/Cole are incredible: they managed to make of even the most fleeting contact a meaningful human encounter, thus turning all the sweat and misery into a continual making of adventure. Terry Hendrix, Kris Lundquist, and Micky Stay, in particular, helped me immensely over the rocky patches. Ingrid Miller did most of the typing and stuff, reminding me often of the inconvenience of a world without women. Finally, Barbara shows me every day that the scientific study of this topic is not really where it's at, and Lisa and Tal, neither of whom was born when this book got started, are rapidly making me eat most of my words. Crunch, peace, crunch.

Dirk L. Schaeffer

Contents

Prologue

We are all students of personality. Because throughout our lives we are intimately involved with other persons, we find it useful and often fascinating to learn as much as possible about those others. To do so, we use a variety of techniques, ranging from elaborate scientific experiments to the basic rudiments of common sense. Yet no matter how much our *tactics* may differ our strategies are always the same. In essence, we look for some relatively easily identified attribute, such as hair color, that is possessed by some, but not all, people; we then try to relate this attribute to another that is not so easily identified, such as temperament. After a number of observations of people who possess those attributes and people who do not, we may conclude that the two attributes are lawfully related; we can then use our knowledge of the first attribute to make inferences about the second. This procedure is useful, scientific, often very interesting, and eminently practical.

For example, college-entrance advisers use knowledge of a student's high school record and entrance examinations (attributes that are relatively easily identified) to predict whether he will succeed in college (an attribute that is totally unknowable when he applies for admission). Similarly, you probably learned at an early age that, when your father frowned in a certain way (easily identified attribute), it meant he was about to swat you (not identifiable until it was too late). Later you learned that members of the opposite sex (still relatively easily identified) had different ideas about how to end an evening on a date (less easily identified) than you did, and you used this knowledge to guide your behavior and expectations in dating situations.

In all these cases we make inferences from knowledge of one attribute to the probable state of another, presumably related, attribute. The science of personality, as a scientific discipline, consists of nothing more than the attempt to identify such pairs of related attributes and to explain how such relationships came about.

The task of labeling these "relatively easily identified" characteristics possessed by some but not all people is known as *taxonomy*, which is at the basis of all sciences. In the last few centuries taxonomy has made great strides in zoology and botany, through the classification of animals and plants according to an evolutionary model, and in chemistry and physics, through identification of the elements according to the periodic table. Unhappily, in the area of psychology, and particularly in the subareas of personality and clinical psychology, taxonomy is in its infancy. Only a few "less easily identified" attributes have been clearly shown to be meaningful dimensions for the classification of persons. Although psychologists have attempted to isolate such dimensions as anxiety, authoritarianism, and need for achievement, only one—intelligence—has been generally accepted and widely applied outside the realm of psychology itself.

Other personal attributes can be considered. An obvious and quite useful one is age, which leads to wide differences in other attributes. As an example, compare the behavior of your father and your 10-year-old nephew in almost any situation. People also differ in height, weight, and hair color, but these attributes do not seem to be consistently related to personality characteristics. Even skin color, a very obvious attribute that has for millennia been used to separate people for special treatment, turns out to be quite probably unrelated to personality characteristics *except* as it affects the way one is treated by others. That is, differential treatment may lead to differences in personality formation.

In this text we will concentrate our attention on the attribute of sex. Although anatomical or physiological sex differences are quite obvious, they may or may not be basic in their effects on personality. That is, the differences in personality functions that undeniably exist between the sexes may be directly traceable to the anatomical, hormonal, and other physiological differences between men and women. On the other hand, these differences may stem from indirect factors, such as the differential treatment that boys and girls receive in most societies. The selections in this book will explore both these possibilities.

The serious study of sex differences in personality, ability, and behavior is less than a hundred years old, although both occupational and status segregation of the sexes is as old as history. Woman's lesser strength and greater dependency (particularly during and just after pregnancy) have tended to force her into a passive, dependent role close to the campfire; the less burdened male has gone hunting. This difference has been taken for granted in most societies and seldom questioned or investigated. Plato, however, believed that the only difference between the sexes was that women were weaker. In *The Republic*, he commented that, since female dogs were not segregated from male dogs in hunting or keeping watch, female humans should not be denied similar functions. He then proposed that women would best be able to serve as "guardians" for his utopian Republic. But few persons accepted the validity of Plato's arguments. For centuries society continued to see women as different from men—probably inferior, certainly weaker, and only in rare qualities superior.

Toward the end of the 12th century, woman began to emerge from her inferior position. Andreas Capellanus, a chaplain in the court of Eleanor of Aquitaine, wrote a booklet entitled "The Art of Courtly Love." In this manual for upper-class romantics, he glorified women as being equal or even superior to men in the art of love. As a result of this new attitude, woman began to enjoy a position far superior to that which she had held previously.

However, Capellanus' arguments proved even more fleeting than Plato's, since Andreas himself denounced them after he escaped from Eleanor's immediate influence. Woman's role remained more or less unchanged (that is, more or less inferior) until the advent of the Industrial Revolution. Although machines magnified the distinction between home and work and thus created an even wider separation of the sexes, they also offered women a chance to expand their capacities, so that their physical weakness no longer appeared so important. In about the middle of the 19th century, women joined the labor force, and their serious struggle for rights began. They have progressively achieved the vote, education, and—with the help of Freud and the Pill —a measure of sexual equality.

It was not until this movement for female equality was well under way that philosophers and scientists began seriously to investigate the psychological differences between men and women. The pioneer theorist in this area was Havelock Ellis, who was concerned with sex differences and intelligence. In about 1905 he observed that, although half the people in the world were female, an infinitesimally small fraction of *famous* people were female. Those women who achieved fame usually did so by accident of birth or marriage, rather than by independent achievement. Moreover, Ellis observed that a far larger number of mental defectives and inmates of mental institutions were male than female. From these two facts—the lesser achievement of females and the greater insanity of males—he wove an ingenious theory.

Ellis proposed, in essence, that males and females were *in general* equal in all characteristics but that men were *more variable* than women. Thus, although extreme cases would balance each other out, *some* men would typically be more intelligent than *any* women, and some other men would typically be less intelligent than any women. Equally, with any other characteristic—height, weight, charm, talent, ability to calculate square roots mentally—*some* men would always prove to be better than *any* women and some worse.

This beautiful theory accounted for virtually all the differences that had been observed between the sexes. But less than 20 years after Ellis propounded it, Leta Hollingsworth hypothesized, after intensively investigating the mentally defective, that it was not innate capacity but differential social treatment that led more men than women to be institutionalized. Because society made fewer demands on women, a mentally defective female could stay at home as a reasonably adequate cook, housekeeper, and breeder of children; an equally defective male, unable to perform adequately outside the home, would be more likely to be institutionalized. Similarly, Hollingsworth explained the lesser achievement of the female as a result of societal expectations and prohibitions.

Shortly thereafter Freud's theories of psychosexual development appeared. He argued that it was the childhood experience of the anatomical distinction between the sexes, as well as its consequences, that played a critical role in the formation of adult personality. Thus Freud's explanation for sex differences was both more sophisticated than the simple statement that they exist and more meaningful than the attempt to trace them all to the effects of different socialization experiences. Freud did allow for the effects of learning and specific socialization experiences. However, the most significant aspect of his theory was that *some* kinds of learning are virtually *inevitable*—that is, a boy *must* experience castration anxiety and the Oedipus complex, simply because he has a penis; a girl *must* experience penis envy and resentment of her mother, simply because she lacks a penis. Moreover, this kind of "learning" is quite different from that usually dealt with by academic psychologists, since it is neither cognitive nor conscious but rather affective (emotional) and unconscious.

These two theories—Hollingsworth's social learning and Freud's psychosexual developmental—each offered a meaningful and potentially comprehensive explanation for observed sex differences. Their wide areas of disagreement offered fertile field for other psychologists to examine them by means of statistical and empirical tests, to elaborate on them, to attempt to reconcile them, and to propose intermediates. As a result, we have a rich and elaborate literature of sex differences.

Of course, it is now an oversimplification to hold solely to either one of these positions. Many theorists (such as C. G. Jung, Karen Horney, and Talcott Parsons) have proposed intermediate positions, representing either a "socialization" of pure Freudianism or a "sexualization" of pure social learning positions. Cross-cultural evidence, such as that collected by Bronislaw Malinowski, Ruth Benedict, and Margaret Mead, strongly suggests that many of the Freudian principles are not so universal as was believed, although certain regularities in sex-role patterns appear to transcend the immediate effects of any given society.

Both Freud and the early social learning theorists based most of their arguments on certain implicit *assumptions* about the nature of sex differences. They "knew" that males are active, females passive; males aggressive, females submissive; males strong, females weak; males innately polygamous, females monogamous. Scheinfeld (1943) has summarized most of these differences and has attempted, on a purely speculative level, to trace them to their biological origins (see Table 1).

Recently, however, many of these assumptions about innate personality differences between the sexes have been experimentally tested to determine if they indeed exist and, if so, to what prior life experiences they may be related. It turns out, for example, that males really are more aggressive than females in most situations; yet females can be equally ambitious when the proper motivators are used (McClelland, 1964). Although many of the data uncovered by these experiments can be used to support either a social learning or a Freudian viewpoint, the majority of investigators today would feel uncomfortable with such a strict division; they tend to reject simple, all-embracing theories in favor of more modest "local" theories (for example, of identification or aggression) that involve sex differences as only one of their components. Nevertheless, approaching the data on sex differences from the standpoint of two competing theories may allow for a more meaningful organization of the material, and the discussions in this text will often adopt this approach. Neither theory should be expected to be correct all the time.

In addition to these two theoretical positions, there is a third approach to sex differences in personality. It is a little more difficult to classify and organize, but it may in fact represent the most common orientation to this research area. This is the simple search for empirical data bearing on such differences. The line of reasoning involved is a straightforward extension of the basic strategy cited above: sexuality is an easily identified attribute, and it is both perfectly reasonable and quite simple to determine how the sexes differ on any given personal-

Table 1. Some "Biosocial" Factors and How They Work to Accentuate Sex Differences.

Biological Sex Differences	Intermediate Results	Social Sex Differences
Men stronger, bigger.	Greater capacity for heavy labor.	Different jobs, roles, assigned to each sex; in anticipation, different training given to each.
Women bear children, nurse them. Pregnancy in women.	Movements impeded, kept closer to home. Greater risk in sexual relationships, uncertainty of paternity. Bad habits may affect children.	"Double standard" of conduct, stricter codes for behavior of unmarried girls and married women.
Earlier puberty in girls.	Ready for mating earlier.	Girls permitted to marry, reach "age of consent" earlier.
Differences in genitalia and body form.	Garments adjusted differently for comfort, utility.	Differences in dress, styles.
Instinct of males not to fight females. Menstruation.	Need of men to treat women differently. Effects on body, mind, consciousness of blood issue, other symptoms.	Codes of chivalry, etiquette. Taboos on women, psychological and social restraints.
Greater muscular development in males. Male's larger size, higher metabolism, greater activity.	Urge to physical exertion, pride in it. Need for more food, more expenditure of energy.	Greater interest of male in sports, etc. Greater drive in work, achievement.
Lesser strength of female.	Inability to cope with male physically.	Round-about "feminine" device to achieve ends.
Roles in sexual relationships.	Women can have intercourse without desire, men cannot.	Prostitution confined to women, rape to men.
Menopause in women.	Reproductive capacity ends much earlier than men's.	Men's marriage chances continue beyond women's.
Female biologically more resistant to disease, bodily upsets.	Her life-span longer, woman-surplus growing.	Threat to monogamous marriage system; problems of widowhood.
Women dependent during childbearing, nursing.	Expedient to wait for man to offer protection and support.	Men propose marriage.

From A. Scheinfeld, *Women and Men.* New York: Harcourt, Brace, 1943. Reprinted by permission.

ity test. It is so simple, in fact, that Goldberg (1970) has recently argued that sex differences may be one of the most trivially done-to-death personality dimensions ever investigated. He maintains that the ease of doing such a study has blinded experimenters to the fact that their results just may be meaningless in the absence of any theoretical superstructure to which to relate their findings.

Historically this form of investigation received its major impetus from the work of Lewis Terman (Terman & Miles, 1936), who, like Havelock Ellis earlier, seemed equally torn between investigations of intelligence and sexuality. To Terman's credit it must be stated that he did *not* merely investigate the differences in the responses of males and females to unselected test items, but rather set out to develop a test that would both highlight those differences and identify their underlying dimensions. In the former task he succeeded admirably; the seven-part Terman-Miles Attitude-Interest Inventory shows less overlap across sexes than any other test devised. But the latter task seems to have eluded him as it did most other investigators.

But nothing spoils like success. Since Terman, virtually every objective personality test devised has contained a masculinity-femininity scale, has offered separate norms for males and females, or has done both. Despite the vast accumulation of research results that have grown out of this approach, it seems fair to say, with Goldberg, that we have learned almost nothing from all these data that we could not have learned from Terman himself.

One

Perception of the Self and Others

The readings in this section deal primarily with the ways in which males and females see themselves, simply because they are males and females, and with some of the differences that result from these perceptions. Since, in a very real sense, one is what one believes and believes what one sees, this differential perception may lie at the core of the question of sex differences in personality.

The first two selections present, respectively, Freud's most precise summary of his psychosexual developmental position, as it affects sex differences, and Gerald Blum's findings with the Blacky Test, which support Freud's position. The next pair of readings concern the social learning theory. David Lynn's concise statement summarizes several years of study, and Jerome Kagan's deceptively simple study points to the pervasiveness of socially learned sex distinctions.

The last two selections deal with sex stereotyping—that is, the tendency to classify persons into certain stereotypical roles on the basis of gender. Although this tendency is at the base of all personality study—formal or informal—many aspects of these stereotypes may not be conscious. Caroline MacBrayer and Philip Goldberg shed some light on what these stereotypes consist of in our society and how they operate.

Space restrictions have made it impossible to include in this section Kohlberg's "Cognitive-developmental analysis of children's sex-role concepts and attitudes" (1966), which is probably the most carefully elaborated statement of the social learning position on the development of sex differences; and Bennett and Cohen's "Men and women, personality patterns and contrasts" (1959), which is, next to Terman's work, probably the most extensive and meaningful summary of sex differences in personality. Kohlberg's study consists of a careful reanalysis of a large number of experiments in the development of sex differences. It cannot easily be summarized. However, the Bennett and Cohen study should be briefly described.

These investigators presented a series of 300 words, in groups of 15, to their subjects and asked them to identify those words that described them best, second best, third best, and so on, until the entire list was exhausted. (For words with high social-desirability value, subjects were asked to identify first those words that described them *least*, second least, and so on.) The words dealt with the individual's wishes, values, and social environment. The subject pool consisted of 1,300 people, aged 15 to 64, and was weighted to produce a distribution comparable to that of the 1950 U.S. census. (Thus this study is one of the few in this area that did not use either college students or schoolchildren as subjects.) Bennett and Cohen summarized their results in terms of five general principles reflecting the nature of sex differences. Although they describe each principle in terms of their subjects' "thinking," a phrase such as "value system" may perhaps more meaningfully (if less scientifically) identify the principle involved.

1. Masculine thinking is a modification downward in intensity of feminine thinking.
2. Masculine thinking is oriented more in terms of the self, while feminine thinking is oriented more in terms of the environment.
3. Masculine thinking anticipates rewards and punishments determined more as a result of the adequacy or inadequacy of the self, while feminine thinking anticipates rewards and punishments determined more as a result of the friendship or hostility of the environment.
4. Masculine thinking is associated more with desire for personal achievement, while feminine thinking is associated more with desire for social love and friendship.
5. Masculine thinking finds value more in malevolent and hostile actions against a competitive society, while feminine thinking finds value more in freedom from restraint in a friendly and pleasant environment.

Sigmund Freud

Some Psychological Consequences of the Anatomical Distinction between the Sexes

A major virtue of Freud's theory of psychosexual development (the oral-anal-phallic-latency sequence and the Oedipus complex) is that it both demands and accounts for extensive sex differences in adult personality; moreover, it derives these differences from the incontrovertible biological distinctions between the sexes. Social learning theories, on the other hand, can account for sex differences but neither demand them nor offer any *ultimate* explanation for them. That is, they explain how sex differences continue to be propagated but seldom how they initially arose.

Nevertheless, Freud's theory is not entirely free of difficulties. Whereas social learning theorists find it difficult to explain male identification (since throughout his early years the child has far more contact with his mother than with his father), Freudians have difficulties with females. For example, although it is critical for the development of mature female sexuality that the girl transfer her envious wish for a penis into the wish for a child, Freud is not able to explain *how* this transfer comes about—it just does. Similarly, Freud's suggestion that males *must* see females as objects to be either pitied or scorned simply does not

agree with our intuitive notions of how we feel about most of the females we know. It might be better to admit the transfer of many of the positive feelings the infant develops for his mother to later adult relations, along with the pity or scorn. However, in this selection Freud avoids this complexity and ambivalence.

This article is the second of a series of three that Freud wrote in elaboration of his theory of childhood sexuality, which he first presented in *Three Essays on the Theory of Sexuality* (1905a). The other two in this series are "The Passing of the Oedipus Complex" (1924) and "Female Sexuality" (1931).

In the selection reprinted here, Freud, besides discussing the direct consequences of the differences between the sexes, formulates several quite specific hypotheses about more general personality differences resulting from the anatomical distinctions. Although he indicates that he is not entirely sure of the validity of many of these hypotheses, subsequent research has provided more detailed experimental results.

1. Freud suggests that both males and females perceive females as inferior. The studies by Mac-

Chapter XVII of Volume 5 of *The Collected Papers of Sigmund Freud*, edited by Ernest Jones, M. D. Basic Books, Inc., Publishers, New York, 1959.

Brayer (pp. 56-61) and Goldberg (pp. 62-66) are only two of the many that document this point.

2. Freud suggests that females have a weaker superego than males. Hall's short paper (pp. 79-82) neatly supports this point.

3. Freud suggests that females identify with the mother less than males identify with the father. Blum (pp. 22-40) presents evidence for this hypothesis in the results obtained with his Blacky Test; on the other hand, some of the evidence presented by Lynn (pp. 41-49) would seem to refute it.

4. Freud suggests that females are more jealous than males. However, jealousy apparently has not been investigated by psychologists.

5. Freud suggests that masturbation, particularly during puberty, is far less common in girls than in boys. Kinsey's data (Kinsey, Pomeroy, Martin, & Gebhard, 1953) show that less than two-thirds of his adult female sample (62%) reported ever having masturbated, whereas almost all adult males (93%) masturbate. This difference is most marked during puberty, when only 8% of girls but 61% of boys have their first masturbatory experience.

Thus roughly four of the five predictions Freud makes have found empirical support suggesting that his theory may be on fairly safe ground. In all the experiments that confirmed Freud's hypotheses, the subjects were 20th-century Americans; this fact suggests that Freud's hypotheses are *not*, as some critics have argued, relevant only to 19th-century Viennese.

Some of Freud's terminology may appear a little formidable to the reader not initiated into psychoanalytic jargon. Basically, Freud developed this article from his theory of psychosexual development, which postulates several rudimentary, childhood precursors of mature (genital) sexuality; the oral, anal, phallic, and latency periods, during which the child derives sensual pleasure from his mouth, anus, external genitalia, and nothing at all, respectively. The child cathects, or invests much libidinal energy in, any object or person associated with gratification in these three areas. During the oral and anal stages these cathexes do not present many problems. However, when the child enters the phallic stage, new, intense problems arise from society's taboos against masturbation and from the Oedipus conflict, in which the boy rather naively wishes to use his new-found source of pleasure, the penis, to please his oldest source of pleasure, the mother. He consequently becomes resentful of his father. The child escapes these problems by renouncing his sexual desires and entering the latency stage, which lasts until the hormonal pressures of mature sexuality force him to face these problems again during puberty and adolescence.

In my own writings and in those of my followers more and more stress is laid upon the necessity for carrying the analyses of neurotics back into the remotest period of their childhood, the time of the early efflorescence of sexual life. It is only by examining the first manifestations of the patient's innate instinctual constitution and the effects of his earliest experiences that we can accurately gauge the motive forces that have led to his neurosis and can be secure against the errors into which we might be tempted by the degree to which they have become remodelled and overlaid in adult life. This requirement is not only of theoretical but also of practical importance, for it distinguishes our efforts from the work of those physicians whose interests are focussed exclusively upon therapeutic results and who employ analytic methods, but only up to a certain point. An analysis of early childhood such as we are considering is tedious and laborious and makes demands both upon the physician and upon the patient which cannot always be met. Moreover it leads us into dark regions where there are as yet no sign-posts. Indeed, analysts may feel reassured, I think, that there is no risk of their work becoming mechanical, and so of losing its interest, during the next few decades.

In the following pages I bring forward some findings of analytical research which would be of great importance if they could be proved to apply universally. Why do I not postpone publication of them until further experience has given me the necessary proof, if such proof is obtainable? Because the conditions under which I work have undergone a change, with implications which I cannot disguise. Formerly, I was never one of those who are unable to hold back what seems to be a new discovery until it has been either confirmed or corrected. My *Interpretation of Dreams* (1900) and my "Fragment of an Analysis of a Case of Hysteria" (1905b) (the case of Dora) were suppressed by me—if not for the nine years enjoined by Horace—at all events for four or five years before I allowed them to be published. But in those days I had unlimited time before me and material poured in upon me in such quantities that fresh experiences were hardly to be escaped. Moreover, I was the only worker in a new field, so that my reticence involved no danger to myself and no risk of loss to others.

But now everything has changed. The time before me is limited. The whole of it is no longer spent in working, so that my opportunities for making fresh observations are not so numerous. If I think I see something new, I am uncertain whether I can wait for it to be confirmed. And further, everything that is to be seen upon the surface has already been exhausted; what remains has to be slowly and laboriously dragged up from the depths. Finally, I am no longer alone. An eager crowd of fellow-workers is ready to make use of what is unfinished or doubtful, and I can leave to them that part of the work which I should otherwise have done myself. On this occasion, therefore, I feel justified in publishing something which stands in urgent need of confirmation before its value or lack of value can be decided.

In examining the earliest mental shapes assumed by the sexual life of children we have been in the habit of taking as the subject of our investigations the male child, the little boy. With little girls, so we have supposed, things must be similar, though in some way or other they must nevertheless be different. The point in development at which this difference lay could not clearly be determined.

In boys the situation of the Oedipus complex is the first stage that can be recognized with certainty. It is easy to understand, because at that stage a child retains the same object which he previously cathected with his pregenital libido during the preceding period while he was being suckled and nursed. The further fact that in this situation he regards his father as a disturbing rival and would like to get rid of him and take his place is a straightforward consequence of the actual state of affairs. I have shown elsewhere how the Oedipus attitude in little boys belongs to the phallic phase, and how it succumbs to the fear of castration, that is, to narcissistic interest in their own genitals. The matter is made more difficult to grasp by the complicating circumstance that even in boys the Oedipus complex has a double orientation, active and passive, in accordance with their bisexual constitution; a boy also wants to take his *mother's* place as the love-object of his *father*—a fact which we describe as the feminine attitude.

As regards the prehistory of the Oedipus complex in boys we are far from complete clarity. We know that that period includes an identification of an affectionate sort with the boy's father, an identification which is still free from any sense of rivalry in regard to his mother. Another element of that stage is invariably, I believe, a masturbatory stimulation of the genitals, the masturbation of early childhood, the more or less violent suppression of which by the persons in charge of the child sets the castration complex in action. It is to be assumed that this masturbation is attached to the Oedipus complex and serves as a discharge for the sexual excitation belonging to it. It is, however, uncertain whether the masturbation has this character from the first, or whether on the contrary it makes its first appearance spontaneously as an activity of a bodily organ and is only brought into relation with the Oedipus complex at some later date; this second possibility is by far the more probable. Another doubtful question is the part played by bed-wetting and by the breaking of that habit through the intervention of training measures. We are inclined to adopt the simple generalization that continued bed-wetting is a result of masturbation and that its suppression is regarded by boys as an inhibition of their genital activity, that is, as having the meaning of a threat of castration; but whether we are always right in supposing this remains to be seen. Finally, analysis shows us in a shadowy way how the fact of a child at a very early age listening to his parents copulating may set up his first sexual excitation, and how that event may, owing to its after-effects, act as a starting-point for the child's whole sexual development. Masturbation, as well as the two attitudes in the Oedipus complex, later on become attached to this early experience, the child having subsequently interpreted its meaning. It is impossible, however, to suppose that these observations of coitus are of universal occurrence, so that at this point we are faced with the problem of "primal phantasies." Thus the prehistory of the Oedipus complex, even in boys, raises all of these questions for sifting and explanation; and there is the further problem of whether we are to suppose that the process invariably follows the same course, or whether a great variety of different preliminary stages may not converge upon the same terminal situation.

In little girls the Oedipus complex raises one problem more than in boys. In both cases the mother is the original object; and there is no cause for surprise that boys retain that object in the Oedipus complex. But how does it happen that girls abandon it and instead take their father as an object? In pursuing this question I have been able to reach some conclusions which may throw light upon the prehistory of the Oedipus relation in girls.

Every analyst has come across certain women who cling with especial intensity and tenacity to the bond with their father and to the wish in which it culminates of having a child by him. We have good reason to suppose that the same wishful phantasy was also the motive force of their infantile masturbation, and it is easy to form an impression that at this point we have been brought up against an elementary and unanalysable fact of infantile sexual life. But a thorough analysis of these very cases brings something different to light, namely, that here the Oedipus complex has a long prehistory and is in some respects a secondary formation.

The old paediatrician Lindner once remarked that a child discovers the genital zones (the penis or the clitoris) as a source of pleasure while indulging in sensual sucking (thumb-sucking)[1]: I shall leave it an open question whether it is really true that the child takes the newly found source of pleasure in exchange for the recent loss of the mother's nipple—a possibility to which later phantasies (fellatio) seem to point. Be that as it may, the genital zone is discovered at some time or other, and there seems no justification for attributing any psychical content to its first stimulations. But the first step in the phallic phase which begins in this way is not the linking-up of the masturbation with the object-cathexes of the Oedipus situation, but a

---

[1]Cf. *Three Essays on the Theory of Sexuality* (1905a).

momentous discovery which little girls are destined to make. They notice the penis of a brother or playmate, strikingly visible and of large proportions, at once recognize it as the superior counterpart of their own small and inconspicuous organ, and from that time forward fall a victim to envy for the penis.

There is an interesting contrast between the behaviour of the two sexes. In the analogous situation, when a little boy first catches sight of a girl's genital region, he begins by showing irresolution and lack of interest; he sees nothing or disowns what he has seen, he softens it down or looks about for expedients for bringing it into line with his expectations. It is not until later, when some threat of castration has obtained a hold upon him, that the observation becomes important to him: if he then recollects or repeats it, it arouses a terrible storm of emotion in him and forces him to believe in the reality of the threat which he has hitherto laughed at. This combination of circumstances leads to two reactions, which may become fixed and will in that case, whether separately or together or in conjunction with other factors, permanently determine the boy's relations to women: horror of the mutilated creature or triumphant contempt for her. These developments, however, belong to the future, though not to a very remote one.

A little girl behaves differently. She makes her judgement and her decision in a flash. She has seen it and knows that she is without it and wants to have it.[2]

From this point there branches off what has been named the masculinity complex of women, which may put great difficulties in the way of their regular development towards femininity, and it cannot be got over soon enough. The hope of some day obtaining a penis in spite of everything and so of becoming like a man may persist to an incredibly late age and may become a motive for the strangest and otherwise unaccountable actions. Or again, a process may set in which might be described as a "denial," a process which in the mental life of children seems neither uncommon nor very dangerous but which in an adult would mean the beginning of a psychosis. Thus a girl may refuse to accept the fact of being castrated, may harden herself in the conviction that she *does* possess a penis and may subsequently be compelled to behave as though she were a man.

The psychical consequences of penis-envy, in so far as it does not become absorbed in the reaction-formation of the masculinity com-

[2]This is an opportunity for correcting a statement which I made many years ago (Freud, 1905a). I believed that the sexual interest of children, unlike that of pubescents, was aroused, not by the differences between the sexes, but by the problem of where babies come from. We now see that, at all events with girls, this is certainly not the case. With boys it may no doubt happen sometimes one way and sometimes the other; or with both sexes chance experiences may determine the event.

plex, are various and far-reaching. After a woman has become aware of the wound to her narcissism, she develops, like a scar, a sense of inferiority. When she has passed beyond her first attempt at explaining her lack of a penis as being a punishment personal to herself and has realized that that sexual character is a universal one, she begins to share the contempt felt by men for a sex which is the lesser in so important a respect, and, at least in the holding of that opinion, insists upon being like a man.[3]

Even after penis-envy has abandoned its true object, it continues to exist: by an easy displacement it persists in the character-trait of *jealousy*. Of course, jealousy is not limited to one sex and has a wider foundation than this, but I am of opinion that it plays a far larger part in the mental life of women than of men and that that is because it is enormously reinforced from the direction of displaced penis-envy. While I was still unaware of this source of jealousy and was considering the phantasy "A Child Is Being Beaten" (1919), which occurs so commonly in girls, I constructed a first phase for it in which its meaning was that another child, a rival of whom the subject was jealous, was to be beaten. This phantasy seems to be a relic of the phallic period in girls. The peculiar rigidity which struck me so much in the monotonous formula "a child is being beaten" can probably be interpreted in a special way. The child which is being beaten (or caressed) may at bottom be nothing more nor less than the clitoris itself, so that at its very lowest level the statement will contain a confession of masturbation, which has remained attached to the content of the formula from its beginning in the phallic phase up to the present time.

A third consequence of penis-envy seems to be a loosening of the girl's relation with her mother as a love-object. The situation as a whole is not very clear, but it can be seen that in the end the girl's mother, who sent her into the world so insufficiently equipped, is almost always held responsible for her lack of a penis. The way in which this comes about historically is often that soon after the girl has discovered that her genitals are unsatisfactory she begins to show jeal-

---

[3]In my first critical account of the "History of the Psychoanalytic Movement," written in 1914 (1914b), I recognized that this fact represents the core of truth contained in Adler's theory. That theory has no hesitation in explaining the whole world by this single point ("organ inferiority," "the masculine protest," breaking away from "the feminine line") and prides itself upon having in this way robbed sexuality of its importance and put the desire for power in its place. Thus the only organ which could claim to be called "inferior" without any ambiguity would be the clitoris. On the other hand, one hears of analysts who boast that, although they have worked for dozens of years, they have never found a sign of the existence of a castration complex. We must bow our heads in recognition of the greatness of this achievement, even though it is only a negative one, a piece of virtuosity in the art of overlooking and mistaking. The two theories form an interesting pair of opposites: in one of them not a trace of a castration complex, in the other nothing at all but its effects.

ousy of another child on the grounds that her mother is fonder of it than of her, which serves as a reason for her giving up her affectionate relation to her mother. It will fit in with this if the child which has been preferred by her mother is made into the first object of the beating-phantasy which ends in masturbation.

There is yet another surprising effect of penis-envy, or of the discovery of the inferiority of the clitoris, which is undoubtedly the most important of all. In the past I had often formed an impression that in general women tolerate masturbation worse than men, that they more frequently fight against it and that they are unable to make use of it in circumstances in which a man would seize upon it as a way of escape without any hesitation. Experience would no doubt elicit innumerable exceptions to this statement, if we attempted to turn it into a rule. The reactions of human individuals of both sexes are of course made up of masculine and feminine traits. But it appeared to me nevertheless as though masturbation were further removed from the nature of women than of men, and the solution of the problem could be assisted by the reflection that masturbation, at all events of the clitoris, is a masculine activity and that the elimination of clitoral sexuality is a necessary pre-condition for the development of femininity. Analyses of the remote phallic period have now taught me that in girls, soon after the first signs of penis-envy, an intense current of feeling against masturbation makes its appearance, which cannot be attributed exclusively to the educational influence of those in charge of the child. This impulse is clearly a forerunner of the wave of repression which at puberty will do away with a large amount of the girl's masculine sexuality in order to make room for the development of her femininity. It may happen that this first opposition to auto-erotic stimulation fails to attain its end. And this was in fact the case in the instances which I analyzed. The conflict continued, and both then and later the girl did everything she could to free herself from the compulsion to masturbate. Many of the later manifestations of sexual life in women remain unintelligible unless this powerful motive is recognized.

I cannot explain the opposition which is raised in this way by little girls to phallic masturbation except by supposing that there is some concurrent factor which turns her violently against that pleasurable activity. Such a factor lies close at hand in the narcissistic sense of humiliation which is bound up with penis-envy, the girl's reflection that after all this is a point on which she cannot compete with boys and that it would therefore be best for her to give up the idea of doing so. Thus the little girl's recognition of the anatomical distinction between the sexes forces her away from masculinity and masculine masturbation on to new lines which lead to the development of femininity.

So far there has been no question of the Oedipus complex, nor has it up to this point played any part. But now the girl's libido slips into a new position by means—there is no other way of putting it—of the equation "penis = child." She gives up her wish for a penis and puts in place of it a wish for a child: and *with this purpose in view* she takes her father as a love-object. Her mother becomes the object of her jealousy. The girl has turned into a little woman. If I am to credit a single exaggerated analytic instance, this new situation can give rise to physical sensations which would have to be regarded as a premature awakening of the female genital apparatus. If the girl's attachment to her father comes to grief later on and has to be abandoned, it may give place to an identification with him and the girl may thus return to her masculinity complex and perhaps remain fixated in it.

I have now said the essence of what I had to say: I will stop, therefore, and cast an eye over our findings. We have gained some insight into the prehistory of the Oedipus complex in girls. The corresponding period in boys is more or less unknown. In girls the Oedipus complex is a secondary formation. The operations of the castration complex precede it and prepare for it. As regards the relation between the Oedipus and castration complexes there is a fundamental contrast between the two sexes. *Whereas in boys the Oedipus complex succumbs to the castration complex,*[4] *in girls it is made possible and led up to by the castration complex.* This contradiction is cleared up if we reflect that the castration complex always operates in the sense dictated by its subject-matter: it inhibits and limits masculinity and encourages femininity. The difference between the sexual development of males and females at the stage we have been considering is an intelligible consequence of the anatomical distinction between their genitals and of the psychical situation involved in it; it corresponds to the difference between a castration that has been carried out and one that has merely been threatened. In their essentials, therefore, our findings are self-evident and it should have been possible to foresee them.

The Oedipus complex, however, is such an important thing that the manner in which one enters and leaves it cannot be without its effects. In boys (as I have shown at length in the paper to which I have just referred and to which all of my present remarks are closely related) the complex is not simply repressed, it is literally smashed to

[4]Cf. "The Passing of the Oedipus-Complex" (1924).

pieces by the shock of threatened castration. Its libidinal cathexes are abandoned, desexualized and in part sublimated; its objects are incorporated into the ego, where they form the nucleus of the super-ego and give that new structure its characteristic qualities. In normal, or rather in ideal, cases, the Oedipus complex exists no longer, even in the unconscious; the super-ego has become its heir. Since the penis (to follow Ferenczi) owes its extraordinarily high narcissistic cathexis to its organic significance for the propagation of the species, the catastrophe of the Oedipus complex (the abandonment of incest and the institution of conscience and morality) may be regarded as a victory of the race over the individual. This is an interesting point of view when one considers that neurosis is based upon a struggle of the ego against the demands of the sexual function. But to leave the standpoint of individual psychology is not likely to be of any immediate help in clarifying this complicated situation.

In girls the motive for the destruction of the Oedipus complex is lacking. Castration has already had its effect, which was to force the child into the situation of the Oedipus complex. Thus the Oedipus complex escapes the fate which it meets with in boys; it may either be slowly abandoned or got rid of by repression, or its effects may persist far into women's normal mental life. I cannot escape the notion (though I hesitate to give it expression) that for women the level of what is ethically normal is different from what it is in men. Their super-ego is never so inexorable, so impersonal, so independent of its emotional origins as we require it to be in men. Character traits which critics of every epoch have brought up against women—that they show less sense of justice than men, that they are less ready to submit to the great necessities of life, that they are more often influenced in their judgements by feelings of affection or hostility—all these would be amply accounted for by the modification in the formation of their super-ego which we have already inferred. We must not allow ourselves to be deflected from such conclusions by the denials of the feminists, who are anxious to force us to regard the two sexes as completely equal in position and worth; but we shall, of course, willingly agree that the majority of men are also far behind the masculine ideal and that all human individuals, as a result of their bisexual disposition and of cross inheritance, combine in themselves both masculine and feminine characteristics, so that pure masculinity and femininity remain theoretical constructions of uncertain content.

I am inclined to set some value on the considerations I have brought forward upon the psychological consequences of the anatomical distinction between the sexes. I am aware, however, that this opinion can only be maintained if my findings, which are based on a handful of cases, turn out to have general validity and to be typical. If not, they would remain no more than a contribution to our knowledge of the different paths along which sexual life develops.

In the valuable and comprehensive studies upon the masculinity and castration complex in women by Abraham (1921), Horney (1923) and Helene Deutsch (1925) there is much that touches closely upon what I have written but nothing that coincides with it completely, so that here again I feel justified in publishing this paper.[5]

[5]Freud returned to this subject in a later work, "Female Sexuality" (1931).

Gerald S. Blum

A Study of the Psychoanalytic Theory of Psychosexual Development

Blum's interest in Freud's developmental theorizing has expressed itself both in his encyclopedic *Psychoanalytic Theories of Personality* (1953) and in the invention of the only projective personality test designed specifically to assess psychosexual development. The Blacky Test consists of a series of cartoons in which the hero (a dog named Blacky) is shown in a variety of situations seen as prototypical of the conflicts, anxieties, and satisfactions associated with the developmental stages Freud has postulated. Blum, in his attempts to validate this test, focused on the sex differences in development that Freud's theory predicted and measured the extent to which they appeared in the responses of his male and female subjects.

Blum's deductive method has been trenchantly criticized by Seward (1950), who argued that Blum, by examining only those differences that he found to be statistically significant in his study, was considering only a very small and, perhaps biased, part of the theory. In reply to this argument, Blum (1950) reasonably pointed out that the present state of formalization of Freud's theory would not allow more sophisticated procedures. This problem is, of course, very real and fundamental with Freud's thought. That is, although Freud presented and elaborated perhaps the most meaningful insights into the workings of the human psychological apparatus—particularly in the emotional sphere—he never codified or formalized them in such a fashion as to make rigorous experimental tests of his propositions possible. Rapaport (1959), Holt (1966), Rapaport and Gill (1959), Waelder (1960), and, in a way, Blum (1961) have attempted such formalizations for parts of Freud's theory, but their conclusions have not led to particularly incisive experiments. What is worse is that most of these attempts have dealt with the more cognitive or formal aspects of Freud's thought; the developmental theory and the theory of defense mechanisms (which may represent Freud's most important contributions) have been considered in detail only by Blum.

For this reason, perhaps, it sometimes appears that Freudian thinking is being pushed further in such nonpsychological areas as English literature (Leslie Fiedler's *Love and Death in the American Novel*, 1960), history (Norman O. Brown's *Life Against Death*, 1959), and political science (Herbert Marcuse's *Eros and Civilization*, 1955) than it is in psychology. Of course, these other disciplines only need to *use* Freud; psychology's far more difficult task is that of verifying him.

Excerpted from *Genetic Psychology Monographs*, 1949, **39**, 3-99. This selection originally appeared on pages 37-53.

Blum's major attempt at this verification lay in the devising of his Blacky Test. The pictures in this test consist of the following:

A frontispiece showing head shots of Blacky, Papa, Mama, and a spotted, sexually neutral sibling named Tippy. It is labeled "The Adventures of Blacky."

I. Mama lying on her side, nursing Blacky.

II. Blacky actively chewing a dog collar labeled "Mama."

III. A row of doghouses labeled "Papa," "Mama," "Tippy," and "Blacky." Blacky, seen from behind, is scratching dirt between Papa's and Mama's houses. The cartoon is described to subjects as "Here Blacky is relieving himself (herself). . . ."

IV. Papa and Mama holding paws, with valentines in the air above their heads, while Blacky looks on from the side.

V. Blacky licking his genitals. The cartoon is described as "Here Blacky is discovering sex. . . ."

VI. Tippy standing with his (her) tail on a chopping block, with a big knife hovering in the air above it, while Blacky watches from the side.

VII. Blacky, with upraised paw, "scolding" a toy black dog.

VIII. Mama and Papa patting Tippy on the head and smiling at him (her) while Blacky watches from the bushes.

IX. A white "angel" dog, with harp and halo, appearing in a balloon that suggests it is Blacky's fantasy. The angel dog is frowning down at Blacky, who is cringing in terror.

X. Blacky asleep, dreaming of an idealized black male dog.

XI. Blacky asleep, dreaming of an idealized black female dog.

. . . Blacky Test data have revealed numerous areas of sex differences which satisfy a criterion of statistical significance. Explanation in terms of the operation of chance factors alone has been ruled out. The next step is to examine each of the specific differences in regard to its consistency with the psychoanalytic theory of psychosexual development. In accordance with the design of the experiment, only those test results which possess statistical significance are to be evaluated in terms of agreement or disagreement with the theory. All of these obtained differences will be investigated also for possible explanations other than those suggested by the theory. Each area of differences between the sexes, found from the Blacky Test, will be discussed in the following outline form:

Area of sex differences on the Blacky Test.
    1. Evidence from psychoanalytic theory.[1]
    2. Evidence from Blacky Test.
    3. Interpretation of 1 and 2.

[1]For purposes of exposition, the theoretical evidence is presented before the Blacky Test data. The actual procedure was the reverse.

The evidence from psychoanalytic theory (Section 1) will be direct quotations, wherever possible, from Sigmund Freud's own writings and from Otto Fenichel's textbook on psychoanalytic theory which appeared in 1945. In some cases direct evidence will be lacking; for these the author will seek to provide indirect or inferential material. In a few there may be no theoretical sources available at all. The Blacky Test sources (Section 2) will be presented explicitly, along with the level of statistical significance. The interpretation of evidence (Section 3) will be an attempt to collate and evaluate the separate sources, including possible extraneous influences such as test artifacts.

A. Prevalence of Oral Sadism

1. Psychoanalytic Theory

Fenichel maintains that the little girl, as a result of pre-oedipal frustrations by the mother, feels hostile toward her and turns away from the mother to the father. He says:

> The most important experiences that precipitate, facilitate, impede, or form the change of object in girls are disappointments coming from the mother, which cause a turning away from her. Among these, weaning, training for cleanliness, and the birth of siblings have the most important repercussions . . . (Fenichel, 1945, p. 89).

The specifically feminine disappointment accounting for the greater antagonism in females is the lack of a penis, for which the mother is held responsible. Awareness of this lack remobilizes anal and especially oral elements, which are often characteristic of subsequent femininity. Fenichel adds:

> It is understandable that this development is open to many disturbances and that conflicts about the pre-oedipal love for the mother play an important role in the neuroses of women. In normal development, too, the relationship of women to their mothers is more frequently ambivalent than is that of most men to their fathers. Some remnants of the pre-oedipal mother fixation are always found in women . . . (p. 90).

Freud links the little girl's hostility directly to oral frustrations:

> The [girl's] complaint against the mother that harks back furthest, is that she has given the child too little milk, which is taken as indicating a lack of love . . . (Freud, 1933, p. 166).

Thus, psychoanalytic theory would predict oral sadism, which is an expression of pre-oedipal hostility toward the mother, to be more prevalent in females than in males. An interesting corollary is the relationship advanced between oral sadism and manic-depressive psychoses. Fenichel reproduces a chart drawn up by Abraham, in which manic-depressive disorders are described as having their dominant point of fixation in the oral-sadistic stage. Manic-depressive disorders are found to be more common among women.

2. Blacky Test

Significantly more females than males (2 per cent level) chose the oral-sadistic alternative (3) in answer to the following question on Cartoon II:

What will Blacky do next with Mama's collar?
(1)   Get tired of it and leave it on the ground.
(2)   Return it to Mama.
(3)   Angrily chew it to shreds.

3. Interpretation

With respect to the prevalence of oral sadism, the Blacky Test finding supports the theoretical expectation that more females than males retain oral-sadistic tendencies.

B. Oral "Voracity"

1. Psychoanalytic Theory

The theoretical sources do not offer any direct or indirect evidence concerning a possible sex difference in greediness.

2. Blacky Test

Significantly more males than females (5 per cent level) picked the voracious alternative (1) in answer to the following question on Cartoon I:

Which one of the following best describes Blacky?
(1)   He's (she's) a little glutton who never stops eating.
(2)   He's (she's) got a hearty appetite which usually gets satisfied.
(3)   He (she) sometimes doesn't get enough to replace all the energy he (she) burns up.

3. Interpretation

The absence of a theoretical viewpoint in this connection precludes evaluation. Nor can the test finding be interpreted with any degree of confidence, since females may have merely refrained from choosing the alternative more often because of its "unladylike" quality.

C. Repression of Anal Sadism

1. Psychoanalytic Theory

There is no explicit theoretical evidence concerning a sex difference in repression of anal sadism. However, a difference can be inferred from Freud's analysis of "hostile and obscene wit." He equates obscene jokes with anality in the following passage:

> The sexual element which is at the basis of the obscene joke comprises more than that which is peculiar to both sexes, and goes beyond that which is common to both sexes; it is connected with all these things that cause shame, and includes the whole domain of the excrementitious. However, this was the sexual domain of childhood, where the imagination fancied a cloaca, so to speak, within which the sexual elements were either badly or not at all differentiated from the excrementitious. In the whole mental domain of the psychology of the neuroses, the sexual still includes the excrementitious, and it is understood in the old, infantile sense (Freud, 1938, pp. 693-694).

Then he proceeds to comment on the function of obscene humor and its differential effect upon the sexes:

> It now becomes comprehensible what wit accomplishes through this service of its tendency. It makes possible the gratification of a craving (lewd or hostile) despite a hindrance which stands in the way; it eludes the hindrance and so derives pleasure from a source that has been inaccessible on account of the hindrance. The hindrance in the way is really nothing more than the higher degree of culture and education which correspondingly increases the inability of the woman to tolerate stark sex matters. . . . The power which makes it difficult or impossible for the woman, and in a lesser degree for the man, to enjoy unveiled obscenities we call "repression" . . . (p. 696).

In another reference he alludes to the greater repression of aggressiveness in women:

> The repression of their aggressiveness, which is imposed upon women by their constitution and by society . . . (Freud, 1933, p. 158).

These statements suggest, in a rather roundabout fashion, that more females than males might be expected to repress anal-sadistic tendencies.

2. Blacky Test

a. Significantly more females than males (1 per cent level) remained oblivious to the introductory comment on Cartoon III ("Here Blacky is relieving himself [herself]") and gave non-anal stories. In terms of the test, this avoidance is construed as repression.

b. Significantly more males than females (1 per cent level) selected the anal-sadistic alternative (4) in answer to the following question on Cartoon III:

How does Blacky feel about the training he's (she's) been getting?
(1) By relieving himself (herself) in the way he's (she's) been taught, he (she) now has an opportunity to show his (her) family what a good dog he (she) can be.
(2) He (she) feels Mama and Papa are expecting too much of him (her) at this early stage.
(3) He (she) is very happy to have control of himself (herself).
(4) He (she) thinks he's (she's) got Mama and Papa right where he (she) wants them.

3. Interpretation

The test findings, like the theory, suggest more extensive repression among females. This is particularly true of the evidence from the Spontaneous Story. The item from the Inquiry, while conceivably indicating greater repression in the case of the females, might possibly be a reflection of originally more widespread anal sadism among males. The latter source therefore cannot be given as much weight as the Spontaneous Story. Evidences from the culture, whose influence Freud specifically mentions in this connection, tend to reinforce the notion that males are freer to express aggressions in an anal context, e.g., swearing by using anal terms. The intrepid reader might perform his own validation of this point by observing differences between the sexes in reactions to anal-sadistic references.

D. Retention of Pre-Oedipal Types of Object Relationships

1. Psychoanalytic Theory

In the course of psychosexual development, there is normally an advance from the early pre-oedipal type of object relationship, in which the child passively experiences a narcissistic need to be loved, to the more active love-seeking which begins in the oedipal period. Typically, residues of the more primitive fear of losing love are retained in varying extents during the later stages. Psychoanalytic theory holds that these residues are more prominent in the case of the female, as a result of the change of object in girls. When the boy reaches the oedipal phase, he continues his original relationship with the mother; the girl must renounce her maternal ties in favor of the father. The completeness of the change is therefore less likely in females than in males. Excerpts from Fenichel on this topic are:

The fact that in this type of identification there is also a regressive element in love is clearer in women than in men. The passive aim of female sexuality is more closely related to the original aims of incorporation than is the active aim of male sexuality. Therefore, passive sexuality has more archaic features than active sexuality. The aim of being loved is more stressed in women than the aim of loving—the narcissistic need and the dependency on the object are greater (Fenichel, 1945, p. 85).

. . . Some remnants of the pre-oedipal mother fixation are always found in women. There are many women whose masculine love objects have more characteristics of their mother than of their father (p. 90).

. . . analysis shows that other and older fears, above all the fear over loss of love, are stronger in women. . . . (p. 99).

Freud stresses the retention of pre-oedipal attachments in females in the following comments:

. . . The girl's Oedipus complex has long concealed from us the pre-oedipal attachment to her mother which is so important and which leaves behind it such lasting fixations . . . (Freud, 1933, p. 176).

. . . Regression [in women] to fixations at these pre-oedipal phases occur very often . . . (p. 179).

. . . In short, we gain the conviction that one cannot understand women, unless one estimates this *pre-oedipal attachment to the mother* at its proper values (p. 163).

2. Blacky Test

Evidence pertaining to the retention of pre-oedipal types of object relationships is derived from Cartoon IV, in which both pre-oedipal and oedipal responses are possible.

a.   More males than females (1 per cent level) select the oedipal alternative (1), more and more females than males (1 percent level) select the pre-oedipal alternative (2) in answer to the following question:

Which one of the following makes Blacky most unhappy?
    (1)   Papa keeping Mama all to himself (Mama keeping Papa all to herself).
    (2)   The idea that Mama and Papa seem to be ignoring him (her) on purpose.

(3)   He (she) is ashamed watching them make love out in the open.

b.   Significantly more females than males (1 per cent level) prefer to be with the same-sex parent:

Which would make a happier picture?
(1)   Mama left on the outside watching Blacky together with Papa.
(2)   Papa left on the outside watching Blacky together with Mama.

c.   Significantly more males than females (5 per cent level) obtain strong total scores on the dimension of Oedipal Intensity.

3.   Interpretation

Theory and test are in specific agreement concerning the greater retention of pre-oedipal components in female than male object relationships.

E.   Sadistic Conception of the Sex Act

1.   Psychoanalytic Theory

Freud discusses this area as follows:

The third of the typical sexual theories appears in children when through some unforeseen domestic occurrence they witness parental sexual intercourse, concerning which they are then able to obtain only a very incomplete idea. Whatever detail it may be that comes under their observation, whether it is the position of the two people, or the sounds, or certain accessory circumstances, in all cases they arrive at the same conclusion, that is, at what we may call the *sadistic conception of coitus*, seeing in it something that the stronger person inflicts on the weaker by force, and comparing it, especially the boy, to a fight as they know it from their childish play . . . (Freud, 1908, p. 69).

Unfortunately the above statement is ambiguous in its implications for a study of sex difference. It is not clear whether Freud means that the boy is only more likely to compare parental intercourse to a fight or whether he is also more likely to conceive of it as sadistic.

2.   Blacky Test

Significantly more males than females (2 per cent level) chose the sadistic alternative (3) in answer to the following question on Cartoon IV:

What does Blacky suspect is the reason behind the scene he's (she's) watching?
  (1) He (she) suspects Mama and Papa are planning an addition to the family.
  (2) He (she) suspects Mama and Papa are very much in love.
  (3) He (she) suspects Papa is having his own way about things.
  (4) He (she) suspects Mama and Papa are purposely depriving him (her) of attention.

3. Interpretation

Agreement between psychoanalytic theory and Blacky Test cannot be evaluated satisfactorily on this point, inasmuch as the available source material for the theoretical position lacks any clear definition. The test finding suggests that males may be more likely than females to regard sexual intercourse as a sadistic act. It is also possible that the answers to the questions are merely an expression of masculine feelings of dominance rather than of a specific conception of the sex act.

F. Prevalence of Masturbation Guilt

1. Psychoanalytic Theory

No evidence has been found from the writings of either Freud or Fenichel which bears on the question of whether masturbation guilt is more prevalent among males or females.

2. Blacky Test

a. Significantly more males than females (1 per cent level) selected the guiltless alternative (1) in answer to the following question on Cartoon V:

How does Blacky feel here?
  (1) Happy, without a care in the world.
  (2) Enjoying himself (herself), but a little worried.
  (3) Mixed up and guilty.

b. Significantly more males than females (2 per cent level) also picked the guiltless alternative (1) in answer to the following question on Cartoon V:

How might Blacky feel about this situation when he (she) is older?
  (1) Happy, without a care in the world.

(2)   Enjoying himself (herself), but a little worried.
(3)   Mixed up and guilty.
(4)   The situation won't come up again when he (she) is older.

3. Interpretation

This area remains in the realm of speculation. The theory furnishes no information, and the test findings are capable of two opposing interpretations. On the one hand, the results may be taken literally to mean that more females than males possess masturbation guilt. Support for this view stems from the cultural fact that the topic of masturbation tends to be more secretly guarded from discussion by females than by males, and hence possibly is more likely to generate guilt. On the other hand, since these two items are the least disguised, the males conceivably may be selecting the guiltless alternatives in an attempt to deny guilt, which may in actuality be more prevalent among men. The theoretical linking of masturbation guilt with fears of castration and oedipal fantasies may be considered consonant with this position.

G. Identification with Parent of the Same Sex

1. Psychoanalytic Theory

In terms of psychoanalytic theory, the resolution of the Oedipus complex is normally accompanied by an identification process, in which the boy represses his sexual desires for the mother and patterns himself after his powerful rival, the father, whereas the girl gives up her strivings toward the father and patterns herself after the mother. The normal identification therefore is with the parent of the same sex. The suddenness and completeness with which this change takes place differ for the two sexes. Fenichel's discussion of this point follows:

> . . . The boy gives up his sensual and hostile Oedipus wishes because of a castration fear, the intensity of which is due to the hypercathexis of the penis during the phallic phase. The complex, according to Freud, "is smashed to pieces by the shock of threatened castration." In girls, however, it is given up because of fear over loss of love, because of disappointment, shame, and also fear over physical injury. All of these forces are of a lesser dynamic value than castration fear; thus the passing of the Oedipus complex in girls generally comes about in a more gradual and less complete way. . . (Fenichel, 1945, p. 108).

2. *Blacky Test*

Evidence concerning parental identifications is obtained from answers to the following four questions on Cartoon VII:

a. "Who talks like that to Blacky—Mama or Papa or Tippy?"— The males tend to say "Papa" and the females "Mama" (1 per cent level).

b. "Whom is Blacky imitating here—Mama or Papa or Tippy?" —The males tend to pick "Papa" and the females pick "Mama" (1 per cent level).

c. "Whom would Blacky rather pattern himself (herself) after— Mama or Papa or Tippy?"—The males say "Papa," the females "Mama" (1 per cent level).

d. "Blacky's disposition, actually, is most like the disposition of which one—Mama or Papa or Tippy?"—The males pick "Papa," the females pick "Mama" (1 per cent level).

3. *Interpretation*

Psychoanalytic theory and Blacky Test results agree that identification normally occurs with the parent of the same sex.

H. Confusion in Identification Process

1. *Psychoanalytic Theory*

Previously quoted sources (Areas *A,D,G*) have pointed to differences between the sexes in regard to completeness of the identification process. Females are said to remain more ambivalent toward their mothers than males do toward their fathers; they retain more preoedipal elements, which interfere with subsequent development; the change of objects in girls impedes the completeness of the oedipal phase; and the resolution of the Oedipus complex is more gradual and less complete in the case of females. For these reasons, the process by which the female identifies with her mother is considered to be less clear-cut than the process whereby the male identifies with his father. In this connection Freud says:

The mother-identification of the woman can be seen to have two levels, the pre-oedipal, which is based on the tender attachment to the mother and which takes her as a model, and the later one derived from the Oedipus-complex, which tries to get rid of the mother and replace her in her relationship with the father. Much of both remains over for the future. . . (Freud, 1933, p. 183).

2. Blacky Test

Two items from Cartoon VII bear on this topic:

a. "Whom would Blacky rather pattern himself (herself) after—Mama or Papa or Tippy?"—Although the males tend to say "Papa" and the females "Mama," the males are significantly more *decisive* than the females in making their choices; i.e., a greater percentage of males choose "Papa" than females choose "Mama" (1 per cent level).

b. "Whom is Blacky most likely to obey—Mama or Papa or Tippy?"—Both males and females say "Papa" significantly more than "Mama" (1 per cent level).

3. Interpretation

The test findings support the theoretical view that the identification process is less clear-cut in the case of females. The latter are less sure with which parent they seek to identify. The process is further complicated by the fact that the father is regarded by females as a figure more likely to be obeyed than the mother—the theory being that the decisive frustrating agent is a crucial influence in identification (1).

I. Aggression Harbored toward Identified Parent

1. Psychoanalytic Theory

The theoretical position has already been discussed in the preceding section (Area H). Females are said to retain stronger undercurrents of hostility toward their identified parent, the mother, than males do toward the father. Freud makes the following statement:

> The turning away from the mother in females occurs in an atmosphere of antagonism; the attachment to the mother ends in hate. Such a hatred may be very marked and may persist throughout an entire lifetime; it may later on be carefully overcompensated; as a rule, one part of it is overcome while another persists. . . (Freud, 1933, p. 165).

2. Blacky Test

Significantly more females than males (2 per cent level) selected the aggressive, hostile alternative (4) in answer to the following question on Cartoon VII:

What would Blacky have an impulse to do if he (she) were in the position of the toy dog?
- (1) Get frightened and hide.
- (2) Stand there and take it.
- (3) Get mad and sulk.
- (4) Start fighting.

3. Interpretation

On Cartoon VII, which is intended to portray the identification process, the subject (Blacky) presumably behaves toward the toy dog in the same manner as the identified parent behaved toward him (her) in real life. The above question from the Inquiry reverses these roles, with the subject now in his original subservient position. Reactions to this situation are taken to indicate the underlying attitude of the subject toward the parent with whom he has sought to identify himself. Consequently, the test finding is consistent with the theory, since more females do express hostile impulses toward the identified parent.

J. Prevalence of Guilt Feeling

1. Psychoanalytic Theory

Neither Freud nor Fenichel seems to offer a statement concerning the relative prevalence of guilt feelings in males and females. A sex difference may be deduced from Fenichel's description of the genesis of guilt, but it must be recognized that such an extension is a tenuous one. Fenichel links guilt feelings to fear of losing love or narcissistic supplies in the following manner:

> When the ego is sufficiently developed to form a judgment that there is danger of a cessation of essential narcissistic supplies, the aim of its signal, "annihilation may occur," must be to influence objects to furnish these supplies. This state represents the anxiety over loss of love which plays so important a role as a motive for defense. . . .
> . . . The anxiety over loss of love, or rather the anxiety arising out of loss of narcissistic supplies, turns into anxiety over loss of the superego's supplies, and the fear into guilt feelings. . . (Fenichel, 1945, pp.135-136).
> Guilt feeling not only has an oral character in general but an oral-sadistic character in particular. . . (p. 138).

Thus, guilt arises from fear of losing the love of the superego introjects or "internalized" parental providers of narcissistic supplies. Concern over loss of love is said to be more prevalent in woman than in men. The latter are more preoccupied by external fears, which have their prototype in the fear of castration. Physiological and anatomical differences between the sexes also play some part in the divergent development. On this point Fenichel says:

> No doubt this physiological difference [in performance of sexual intercourse] contributes to the prevalent roles of castration fear or fear over loss of love in man and woman respectively. However, this cannot be more than a relatively late secondary contribution. The relative preponderance of the respective fears is established in childhood, long before the first experiences in sexual intercourse (p. 100).

From these observations it may be deduced that females, who have more conflicts over internal deprivations and loss of love, theoretically should show greater evidence of guilt feelings than males do.

2. Blacky Test

a. Significantly more females than males (2 per cent level) obtained strong total scores on the dimension of guilt feelings.

b. Significantly more males than females (1 per cent level) chose the externalized alternative (3) in answer to the following question on Cartoon IX:

> How is Blacky's conscience here?
> (1) His (her) conscience is so strong he's (she's) practically paralyzed.
> (2) His (her) conscience is bothering him (her) somewhat, but he's (she's) mostly afraid of what will be done to him (her).
> (3) He's (she's) hardly bothered at all by his (her) conscience, just afraid of what will be done to him (her).

c. Significantly more females than males (1 per cent level) expressed lasting guilt (1) in answer to the following question on Cartoon IX:

> Do you think Blacky will
> (1) Have this feeling as long as he (she) lives?
> (2) Feel badly every now and then?
> (3) Feel badly for a little while and then go out to play?

3. Interpretation

If the theoretical extension made in Section 1 is a legitimate one, the test findings can be said to support it. The responses indicate that females probably possess stronger guilt, whereas males are more concerned with fears of external harm.

K. Figures Introjected as Superego

1. *Psychoanalytic Theory*

Psychoanalytic theory holds that the superego attains its major development, with the passing of the Oedipus complex, in a process whereby parental standards and prohibitions are incorporated or "introjected" by the child as his own. Fenichel's discussion of this point follows:

> ... It is true that in accordance with the "completeness" of the Oedipus complex, everyone bears features of both parents in his superego. Under our cultural conditions, however, generally for both sexes the fatherly superego is decisive; in women, moreover, a motherly superego is effective as a positive ego ideal... (Fenichel, 1945, p. 104).
> ... However, the sexual differences in the formation of the superego are certainly not the same under different cultural circumstances... (p. 469).

Hence, the superegos of both males and females are expected to show more characteristics of the father than of the mother, though cultural circumstances may alter this pattern.

2. *Blacky Test*

Although the proportions are mixed for both sexes, significantly more males than females attribute fatherly characteristics to the superego, whereas significantly more females than males attribute motherly characteristics to the superego (1 per cent level) in answer to the following question on Cartoon IX: "Which character do the actions of the pointing figure remind Blacky of?"

3. *Interpretation*

Fenichel's analysis of the culture as conducive to the formation of fatherly superegos in women as well as in men is not confirmed by the test data. From the Blacky Test, women tend to have motherly superegos. The cultural implications in this area are necessarily limited by the fact that the female subjects in the experiment cannot be considered representative of American women. Recent emphasis on the growing influence of the mother in family life is consistent with the test finding for the females, however. The theoretical observation that the superego in both sexes contains mixed parental elements is supported by the fact that 31 per cent of the males do attribute motherly characteristics to it, while 29 per cent of the females say the superego figure in the cartoon is reminiscent of "Papa."

L. Reactions to Frustration

1. Psychoanalytic Theory

No references to sex differences in type of reaction to frustration have been found in the theoretical sources.

2. Blacky Test

Significantly more females than males (2 per cent level) select the extra punitive alternative (2), whereas significantly more males than females (1 per cent level) select the impunitive alternative (3) in answer to the following question on Cartoon IX:

Who is really to blame for Blacky's feeling this way?
(1) Himself (herself).
(2) Somebody else.
(3) The situation couldn't be helped.

3. Interpretation

Agreement between theory and test cannot be evaluated in this area. The test results per se suggest that the females in the experimental sample, when frustrated, are more likely to project blame on to others (extrapunitive), while the males show a greater tendency to gloss over the situation (impunitive).

M. Attitudes toward Attaining Ego Ideal

1. Psychoanalytic Theory

Again there seems to be no theoretical evidence relevant to differences between the sexes in attitudes toward attaining the ego ideal, i.e., whether males or females are more hopeful of measuring up to the positive standards which they have adopted as goals.

2. Blacky Test

Significantly more females than males (1 per cent level) chose the pessimistic alternative (3) in answer to the following question on Cartoon X (for males) or Cartoon XI (for females):

> Actually, what are Blacky's chances of growing up to be like the figure in his (her) dream?
> (1) Very good.
> (2) Fair.
> (3) Very poor.

3. Interpretation

The absence of theoretical evidence precludes evaluation in this area also. Interpretation of the test finding, which reveals females to be less hopeful than males of reaching the stature of their ego ideal, must be qualified. At first glance, it seems that the females in this study are more willing than the males to adopt a realistic attitude toward their shortcomings. However, the difference may possibly be attributable to dissimilar conceptions of the ego ideal by the two sexes. Perusal of the female responses in the Spontaneous Story suggests that they are largely concerned with the physical beauty of the ideal cartoon figure, and it may be that the sex difference reflects the degree to which females have reconciled themselves to their own physical charms.

N. Prevalence of Narcissism in Love-Object Relationships

1. Psychoanalytic Theory

Psychoanalytic theory specifically states that narcissism in love-object relationships is more prevalent among females than males. Freud, in this connection, says:

> Further, the comparison of man and woman shows that there are funda-
> mental differences between the two in respect to the type of object-choice,
> although these differences are of course not universal. Complete object-love
> of the anaclitic type is, properly speaking, characteristic of the man. . . . A
> different course is followed in the type most frequently met with in women,
> which is probably the purest and truest feminine type. With the development
> of puberty the maturing of the female sex organs, which up till then have
> been in a condition of latency, seems to bring about an intensification of the

original narcissism, and this is unfavorable to the development of a true object-love... (Freud, 1914a, pp. 45-46).

... We attribute to women a greater amount of narcissism (and this influences their object-choice) so that for them to be loved is a stronger need than to love... (Freud, 1933, p. 180).

The conditions of object-choice in women are often enough made unrecognizable by social considerations. Where that choice is allowed to manifest itself freely, it often occurs according to the narcissistic ideal of the man whom the girl would have liked to be... (p. 181).

Fenichel likewise says:

... The aim of being loved is more stressed in women than the aim of loving—the narcissistic need and the dependency on the object are greater (Fenichel, 1945, p. 85).

2. Blacky Test

Significantly more females than males (1 per cent level) obtained strong total scores on the dimension of Narcissistic Love-Object.

3. Interpretation

The Blacky Test finding supports the theoretical contention that narcissistic love-object relationships are more characteristic of females than of males.

O. Summary

A summary of the data included in this chapter is now in order. The Blacky Test has revealed 14 areas in which the responses of males and females differ significantly. Evidence from the theoretical sources has been available *specifically* in seven of these areas (*A, D, G, H, I, K, N*); *inferentially* in two (*C, J*); and *not at all* in five (*B, E, F, L, M*). One conclusion immediately offers itself: Psychoanalytic theory, as presented by Freud and Fenichel, is incomplete in its treatment of sex differences in psychosexual development. Freud himself recognized this lack in a paper on "The Passing of the Oedipus Complex," written in 1924:

It must be confessed, however, that on the whole our insight into these processes of development in the girl is unsatisfying, shadowy, and incomplete (p. 275).

But what about those areas in which the theory *does* take a stand? The Blacky Test data support psychoanalytic theory in six of the seven areas in which there is specific theoretical evidence, and in both of the areas in which the evidence is inferential. The sole area of disagreement is the test finding that females tend to have motherly rather than fatherly superegos. This departure from Fenichel's stated opinion may very possibly be a reflection of the increasing influence of the mother in American life, in contrast to the patriarchal European society in which psychoanalysis grew up. On the whole, the consonance of theory and test in the areas of sex difference is striking. It remains to be seen whether the syntax of the theory, i.e., the relationships postulated between the dimensions, will receive equal support from the Blacky Test findings.

David B. Lynn

The Process of Learning Parental and Sex-Role Identification

This selection, which represents an extremely cogent and precise summary of much of the work done in this area, may be the most succinct statement of the social learning viewpoint that has appeared in the literature. (A more elaborate, and quite compelling, version of this position is presented by Kohlberg in Maccoby (1966).) The predictions about sex differences made by social learning theories are not so specific as those made by Freud's theory; nevertheless, social learning theories appear to explain much the same material. For example, Freud would maintain that the relatively strong superego of the male is derived from fear of castration; Lynn argues that the boy's relatively abstract identification with the father leads to the same end result. Moreover, Freud's theory, too, leaves room for a great deal of quite specific societal learning. Thus the major distinctions between the two positions may be that (1) Freudians feel that certain learning is virtually inevitable in any society, and (2) social learning theorists are far more concerned than Freud was about the formal nature of the learning process. The first distinction gives Freud's theory a "deterministic" and unalterable character, which many contemporary psychologists may reject simply because it runs counter to theories of human equality. The second distinction leads to a large methodological difference; that is, social learning theorists base their arguments on experimental data, whereas Freudians often prefer to argue by analogy, insight, and example.

The purpose of this paper is to summarize the writer's theoretical formulation concerning identification, much of which has been published piecemeal in various journals. Research relevant to new hypotheses is cited, and references are given to previous publications of this writer in which the reader can find evidence concerning the earlier hypotheses. Some of the previously published hypotheses are considerably revised in this paper and, it is hoped, placed in a more comprehensive and coherent framework.

Journal of Marriage and the Family, 1966, **28**, 466-470. Also presented at the Annual Meeting of the American Orthopsychiatric Association, 1966.

Theoretical Formulation

Before developing specific hypotheses, one must briefly define identification as it is used here. *Parental identification* refers to the internalization of personality characteristics of one's own parent and to unconscious reactions similar to that parent. This is to be contrasted with *sex-role identification*, which refers to the internalization of the role typical of a given sex in a particular culture and to the unconscious reactions characteristic of that role. Thus, theoretically, an individual might be thoroughly identified with the role typical of his own sex generally and yet poorly identified with his same-sex parent specifically. This differentiation also allows for the converse circumstances wherein a person is well identified with his same-sex parent specifically and yet poorly identified with the typical same-sex role generally. In such an instance the parent with whom the individual is well identified is himself poorly identified with the typical sex role. An example might be a girl who is closely identified with her mother, who herself is more strongly identified with the masculine than with the feminine role. Therefore, such a girl, through her identification with her mother, is poorly identified with the feminine role (Lynn, 1962).

Formulation of Hypotheses

It is postulated that the initial parental identification of both male and female infants is with the mother. Boys, but not girls, must shift from this initial mother identification and establish masculine-role identification. Typically in this culture the girl has the same-sex parental model for identification (the mother) with her more hours per day than the boy has his same-sex model (the father) with him. Moreover, even when home, the father does not usually participate in as many intimate activities with the child as does the mother, e.g., preparation for bed, toileting. The time spent with the child and the intimacy and intensity of the contact are thought to be pertinent to the process of learning parental identification (Goodfield, 1965). The boy is seldom if ever with the father as he engages in his daily vocational activities, although both boy and girl are often with the mother as she goes through her household activities. Consequently, the father, as a model for the boy, is analogous to a map showing the major outline but lacking most details, whereas the mother, as a model for the girl, might be thought of as a detailed map.

However, despite the shortage of male models, a somewhat stereotyped and conventional masculine role is nonetheless spelled out for the boy, often by his mother and women teachers in the absence of his father and male models. Through the reinforcement of the culture's highly developed system of rewards for typical masculine-role behavior and punishment for signs of femininity, the boy's early learned identification with the mother weakens. Upon this weakened mother identification is welded the later learned identification with a culturally defined, stereotyped masculine role.

(1)* *Consequently, males tend to identify with a culturally defined masculine role, whereas females tend to identify with their mothers* (Lynn, 1959).

Although one must recognize the contribution of the father in the identification of males and the general cultural influences in the identification of females, it nevertheless seems meaningful, for simplicity in developing this formulation, to refer frequently to *masculine-role identification* in males as distinguished from *mother identification* in females.

Some evidence is accumulating suggesting that (2) *both males and females identify more closely with the mother than with the father*. Evidence is found in support of this hypothesis in a study by Lazowick (1955) in which the subjects were 30 college students. These subjects and their mothers and fathers were required to rate concepts, e.g., "myself," "father," "mother," etc. The degree of semantic similarity as rated by the subjects and their parents was determined. The degree of similarity between fathers and their own children was not significantly greater than that found between fathers and children randomly matched. However, children did share a greater semantic similarity with their own mothers than they did when matched at random with other maternal figures. Mothers and daughters did not share a significantly greater semantic similarity than did mothers and sons.

Evidence is also found in support of Hypothesis 2 in a study by Adams and Sarason (1963) using anxiety scales with male and female high school students and their mothers and fathers. They found that anxiety scores of both boys and girls were much more related to mothers' than to fathers' anxiety scores.

Support for this hypothesis comes from a study in which Aldous and Kell (1961) interviewed 50 middle-class college students and their mothers concerning childrearing values. They found, contrary to their expectation, that a slightly higher proportion of boys than girls shared their mothers' childrearing values.

Partial support for Hypothesis 2 is provided in a study by Gray

*Specific hypotheses are numbered and in italics.

and Klaus (1956) using the Allport-Vernon-Lindzey Study of Values completed by 34 female and 28 male college students and by their parents. They found that the men were not significantly closer to their fathers than to their mothers and also that the men were not significantly closer to their fathers than were the women. However, the women were closer to their mothers than were the men and closer to their mothers than to their fathers.

Note that, in reporting research relevant to Hypothesis 2, only studies of *tested similarity*, not *perceived similarity*, were reviewed. To test this hypothesis, one must measure tested similarity, i.e., measure both the child and the parent on the same variable and compare the similarity between these two measures. This paper is not concerned with perceived similarity, i.e., testing the child on a given variable and then comparing that finding with a measure taken as to how the child thinks his parent would respond. It is this writer's opinion that much confusion has arisen by considering perceived similarity as a measure of parental identification. It seems obvious that, especially for the male, perceived similarity between father and son would usually be closer than tested similarity, in that it is socially desirable for a man to be similar to his father, especially as contrasted to his similarity to his mother. Indeed, Gray and Klaus found the males' perceived similarity with the father to be closer than tested similarity.

It is hypothesized that the closer identification of males with the mother than with the father will be revealed more clearly on some measures than on others. (3) *The closer identification of males with their mothers than with their fathers will be revealed most frequently in personality variables which are not clearly sex-typed*. In other words, males are more likely to be more similar to their mothers than to their fathers in variables in which masculine and feminine role behavior is not especially relevant in the culture.

There has been too little research on tested similarity between males and their parents to presume an adequate test of Hypothesis 3. In order to test it, one would first have to judge personality variables as to how typically masculine or feminine they seem. One could then test to determine whether a higher proportion of males are more similar to their mothers than to their fathers on those variables which are not clearly sex-typed, rather than on those which are judged clearly to be either masculine or feminine. To this writer's knowledge, this has not been done.

It is postulated that the task of achieving these separate kinds of identification (masculine role for males and mother identification for females) requires separate methods of learning for each sex. These separate methods of learning to identify seem to be problem-solving for boys and lesson-learning for girls. Woodworth and Schlosberg differentiate between the task of solving problems and that of learning lessons in the following way:

> With a problem to master the learner must explore the situation and find the goal before his task is fully presented. In the case of a lesson, the problem-solving phase is omitted or at least minimized, as we see when the human subject is instructed to memorize this poem or that list of nonsense syllables, to examine these pictures with a view to recognizing them later (Woodworth & Schlosberg, 1954, p. 529).

Since the girl is not required to shift from the mother in learning her identification, she is expected mainly to learn the mother-identification lesson as it is presented to her, partly through imitation and through the mother's selective reinforcement of mother-similar behavior. She need not abstract principles defining the feminine role to the extent that the boy must in defining the masculine role. Any bit of behavior on the mother's part may be modeled by the girl in learning the mother-identification lesson.

However, finding the appropriate identification goal does constitute a major problem for the boy in solving the masculine-role identification problem. When the boy discovers that he does not belong in the same sex category as the mother, he must then find the proper sex-role identification goal. Masculine-role behavior is defined for him through admonishments, often negatively given, e.g., the mother's and teachers' telling him that he should not be a sissy without precisely indicating what he *should* be. Moreover, these negative admonishments are made in the early grades in the absence of male teachers to serve as models and with the father himself often unavailable as a model. The boy must restructure these admonishments in order to abstract principles defining the masculine role. It is this process of defining the masculine-role goal which is involved in solving the masculine-role identification problem.

One of the basic steps in this formulation can now be taken. (4) *In learning the sex-typical identification, each sex is thereby acquiring separate methods of learning which are subsequently applied to learning tasks generally* (Lynn, 1962).

The little girl acquires a learning method which primarily involves (a) a personal relationship and (b) imitation rather than restructuring the field and abstracting principles. On the other hand, the little boy acquires a different learning method which primarily involves (a) defining the goal (b) restructuring the field, and (c) abstracting principles. There are a number of findings which are consistent with Hypothesis 4, such as the frequently reported greater problem-solving skill of males and the greater field dependence of females (Lynn, 1962).

The shift of the little boy from mother identification to masculine-role identification is assumed to be frequently a crisis. It has been observed that demands for typical sex-role behavior come at an earlier age for boys than for girls. These demands are made at an age when boys are least able to understand them. As was pointed out above, demands for masculine sex-role behavior are often made by women in the absence of readily available male models to demonstrate typical sex-role behavior. Such demands are often presented in the form of punishing, *negative* admonishments, i.e., telling the boy what not to do rather than what to do and backing up the demands with punishment. These are thought to be very different conditions from those in which the girl learns her mother-identification lesson. Such methods of demanding typical sex-role behavior of boys are very poor methods for inducing learning.

(5) *Therefore, males tend to have greater difficulty in achieving same-sex identification than females* (Lynn, 1964).

(6) *Furthermore, more males than females fail more or less completely in achieving same-sex identification, but they rather make an opposite-sex identification* (Lynn, 1961).

Negative admonishments given at an age when the child is least able to understand them and supported by punishment are thought to produce anxiety concerning sex-role behavior. In Hartley's words:

This situation gives us practically a perfect combination for inducing anxiety—the demand that the child do something which is not clearly defined to him, based on reasons he cannot possibly appreciate, and enforced with threats, punishments and anger by those who are close to him (Hartley, 1959, p. 458).

(7) *Consequently, males are more anxious regarding sex-role identification than females* (Lynn, 1964). It is postulated that punishment often leads to dislike of the activity that led to punishment (Hilgard, 1962). Since it is "girl-like" activities that provoked the punishment administered in an effort to induce sex-typical behavior in boys, then, in developing dislike for the activity which led to such punishment, boys should develop hostility toward "girl-like" activities. Also, boys should be expected to generalize and consequently develop hostility toward all females as representatives of this disliked role. There is not thought to be as much pressure on girls as on boys to avoid opposite-sex activities. It is assumed that girls are punished neither so early nor so severely for adopting masculine sex-role behavior.

(8) *Therefore, males tend to hold stronger feelings of hostility*

toward females than females toward males (Lynn, 1964). The young boy's same-sex identification is at first not very firm because of the shift from mother to masculine identification. On the other hand, the young girl, because she need make no shift in identification, remains relatively firm in her mother identification. However, the culture, which is male-dominant in orientation, reinforces the boy's developing masculine-role identification much more thoroughly than it does the girl's developing feminine identification. He is rewarded simply for having been born masculine through countless privileges accorded males but not females. As Brown pointed out:

> The superior position and privileged status of the male permeates nearly every aspect, minor and major, of our social life. The gadgets and prizes in boxes of breakfast cereal, for example, commonly have a strong masculine rather than feminine appeal. And the most basic social institutions perpetuate this pattern of masculine aggrandizement. Thus, the Judeo-Christian faiths involve worshipping God, a "Father," rather than a "Mother," and Christ, a "Son," rather than a "Daughter" (Brown, 1958, p. 235).

(9) *Consequently, with increasing age, males become relatively more firmly identified with the masculine role* (Lynn, 1959).

Since psychological disturbances should, theoretically, be associated with inadequate same-sex identification and since males are postulated to be gaining in masculine identification, the following is predicted: (10) *With increasing age males develop psychological disturbances at a more slowly accelerating rate than females* (Lynn, 1961).

It is postulated that as girls grow older, they become increasingly disenchanted with the feminine role because of the prejudices against their sex and the privileges and prestige offered the male rather than the female. Even the women with whom they come in contact are likely to share the prejudices prevailing in this culture against their own sex (Kitay, 1940). Smith (1939) found that with increasing age girls have a progressively better opinion of boys and a progressively poorer opinion of themselves. (11) *Consequently, a larger proportion of females than males show preference for the role of the opposite sex* (Lynn, 1959).

Note that in Hypothesis 11 the term "preference" rather than "identification" was used. It is *not* hypothesized that a larger proportion of females than males *identify* with the opposite sex (Hypothesis 6 predicted the reverse) but rather that they will show *preference* for the role of the opposite sex. *Sex-role preference* refers to the desire to adopt the behavior associated with one sex or the other or the perception of such behavior as preferable or more desirable.

Sex-role preference should be contrasted with *sex-role identification*, which, as stated previously, refers to the actual incorporation of the role of a given sex and to the unconscious reactions characteristic of that role.

Punishment may suppress behavior without causing its unlearning (Hilgard, 1962). Because of the postulated punishment administered to males for adopting opposite-sex role behavior, it is predicted that males will repress atypical sex-role behavior rather than unlearn it. One might predict, then, a discrepancy between the underlying sex-role identification and the overt sex-role behavior of males. For females, on the other hand, no comparable punishment for adopting many aspects of the opposite-sex role is postulated. (12) *Consequently, where a discrepancy exists between sex-role preference and identification, it will tend to be as follows: Males will tend to show same-sex role preference with underlying opposite-sex identification. Females will tend to show opposite-sex role preference with underlying same-sex identification* (Lynn, 1964). Stated in another way, where a discrepancy occurs both males and females will tend to show masculine-role preference with underlying feminine identification.

Not only is the masculine role accorded more prestige than the feminine role, but males are more likely than females to be ridiculed or punished for adopting aspects of the opposite-sex role. For a girl to be a tomboy does not involve the censure that results when a boy is a sissy. Girls may wear masculine clothing (shirts and trousers), but boys may not wear feminine clothing (skirts and dresses). Girls may play with toys typically associated with boys (cars, trucks, erector sets, and guns), but boys are discouraged from playing with feminine toys (dolls and tea sets). (13) *Therefore, a higher proportion of females than males adopt aspects of the role of the opposite sex* (Lynn, 1959).

Note that Hypothesis 13 refers to *sex-role adoption* rather than *sex-role identification* or *preference*. *Sex-role adoption* refers to the overt behavior characteristic of a given sex. An example contrasting sex-role adoption with preference and identification is an individual who *adopts* behavior characteristic of his own sex because it is expedient, not because he *prefers* it nor because he is so *identified*.

Summary

The purpose of this paper has been to summarize the writer's theoretical formulation and to place it in a more comprehensive and coherent framework. The following hypotheses were presented and discussed:

1. Males tend to identify with a culturally defined masculine role, whereas females tend to identify with their mothers.

2. Both males and females identify more closely with the mother than with the father.

3. The closer identification of males with their mothers than with their fathers will be revealed more frequently in personality variables which are not clearly sex-typed.

4. In learning the sex-typical identification, each sex is thereby acquiring separate methods of learning which are subsequently applied to learning tasks generally.

5. Males tend to have greater difficulty in achieving same-sex identification than females.

6. More males than females fail more or less completely in achieving same-sex identification but rather make an opposite-sex identification.

7. Males are more anxious regarding sex-role identification than females.

8. Males tend to hold stronger feelings of hostility toward females than females toward males.

9. With increasing age, males become relatively more firmly identified with the masculine role.

10. With increasing age, males develop psychological disturbances at a more slowly accelerating rate than females.

11. A larger proportion of females than males show preference for the role of the opposite sex.

12. Where a discrepancy exists between sex-role preference and identification, it will tend to be as follows: Males will tend to show same-sex role preference with underlying opposite-sex identification. Females will tend to show opposite-sex role preference with underlying same-sex identification.

13. A higher proportion of females than males adopt aspects of the role of the opposite sex.

Jerome Kagan   The Child's
                         Sex-Role
                         Classification of
                         School Objects

Kagan has long been associated with the Fels Research Institute, which produces some of the best longitudinal developmental data presently available, and he has become one of the foremost researchers in this area. Basically a social learning theorist, he is interested primarily in the development of *concepts* in children; some of these concepts are associated with sex roles. In this selection he demonstrates in a methodologically sophisticated manner the appearance of very precise sex labels for "neutral" objects in second- and third-grade children. His work points to the pervasiveness of sex labeling in our culture and, by implication, suggests that this very pervasiveness can explain sex differences without the invocation of Freudian principles.

In a similar vein, Hattwick (1937) in her observations of nursery school children, showed that even by the age of 2 1/2, girls have a greater tendency than boys to avoid risks, cry easily, fear strange people, be jealous, shrink from notice, stay near adults, tell fanciful stories, and misrepresent facts. Although many of these behaviors can be predicted from Freudian theory, the important point is that they seem to develop *much earlier* than Freudian psychodynamics would allow. Goodenough (1957), through interviews with parents and young children, showed that parental expectations of different behaviors in boys and girls begin virtually with the birth of the child. This finding suggests that, by the age of 2 1/2, children will have had ample time to learn the appropriate, expected behavior—even without the benefit of the specific anatomical learning that Freud's theory demands.

A fundamental axiom in psychological theory states than an organism with a symbol system usually behaves toward a new situation in a manner that is congruent with the symbolic label applied to that situation. This assumption has prompted many investigators to study the child's symbolic labeling of significant objects in his experience, typically his parents (Emmerich, 1959; Kagan & Lemkin, 1960; Kagan,

Child Development, 1964, 35, 1051-1056. Research supported in part by Grant M-4464 from the National Institute of Mental Health, United States Public Health Service.

Hosken, & Watson, 1961). The present research inquired into the child's labeling of a different set of objects, those associated with school, and asked whether young children had a preference for labeling school as feminine or masculine. It is reasonable to assume that the child's sex-role classification of the school environment governs the degree of motivation he will invest in mastery of academic tasks. For the child should be more highly motivated to master tasks that he perceives as sex-appropriate than those he views as representative of the opposite sex.

Method

Subjects

The Ss were drawn from the second and third grades of two public schools, each located in small towns with similar socioeconomic profiles. There were 121 boys and 119 girls in the second-grade sample and 36 boys and 29 girls in the third-grade sample. The population is primarily middle class for the modal level of educational attainment is high school graduation. Among the fathers, 36 per cent did not graduate from high school, 44 per cent had a high school diploma, and 20 per cent had some college training. The corresponding figures for mothers were 42, 45, and 13 per cent.

Procedure

Each S was seen individually by an adult E.[1] Both a male and a female E saw an equal number of boys and girls. Initially, each S was taught three different nonsense syllables to represent the following three concepts: (a) objects associated with males, (b) objects associated with females, (c) objects associated with farms. The nonsense syllables DEP, ROV, and FAS represented the concepts male, female, and farm, respectively. After S learned these associations, he was shown 19 test pictures, some of which illustrated school objects. The child had to apply one of the three syllables he had learned earlier. The detailed procedure follows.

Learning phase. The E said, "I am going to show you some pictures. These pictures belong to one of three groups. All the pictures in one group are alike or go together in some way. We are going to call

[1]The author expresses his appreciation to Deborah Day, Joseph Albert, and Arnold Projansky, who served as Es.

these groups three crazy words. One group is called DEP, one group is called ROV, and one group is called FAS. First, I want you to learn these three words." (*E* then had *S* repeat the words.) "Now I am going to show you these pictures. Some of the pictures belong to the DEP group, others to the ROV group, and some to the FAS group. You must guess which group they belong to. I will tell you after each trial what the correct answer is. In order to give you a hint I will now show you one of the DEP pictures."

E then showed *S* a picture of a man and said this was a DEP; he then showed a picture of a woman and said this was a ROV; he then showed a picture of a silo and said this was a FAS. *E* then showed *S* 21 pictures, allowed him six seconds to answer, and, if no answer was given, gave him the correct answer. *E* continued to present the 21 pictures in the learning series until *S* had 10 consecutive correct reports. Some of the pictures in the learning series included a man's trousers, a boy, a baseball bat, a man's tie (masculine items); a woman's shoe, sewing machine, lipstick, doll, girl, dress (feminine items); and a chicken, pig, cow, haystack, corn (farm items).

Transfer phase.   After *S* reached a criterion of 10 successive correct items, *E* said, "Now I am going to show you some different pictures and I want you to tell me if they are DEP, ROV, or FAS. Take a guess if you are not sure." *E* presented 19 new picture stimuli and recorded *S*'s response. *E* did not give *S* any answer or praise to these stimuli. The stimuli in the transfer series in the order of administration were:

pencil   page of arithmetic
tree   apple
blackboard with A, B, C on it   school building
lion   alligator
library   school desk
rabbit   cup
child's painting with child's hand   map
  showing   carrot
rowboat   a boy and girl sitting at separate
open book   desks
bird

Results

The distributions of responses to each item were skewed, for most of the objects had a dominant meaning. Table 1 contains the percentage of subjects labeling each of the transfer pictures masculine or feminine. The proportion of "farm" responses can be computed by the reader by subtraction from 100 per cent.

Table 1. Percentage of Subjects Labeling Objects Masculine or Feminine.

| | Grade 2 | | | | Grade 3 | | | |
| | Boys | | Girls | | Boys | | Girls | |
Stimulus	M	F	M	F	M	F	M	F
Pencil	79%	15%	61%	36%	81%	11%	79%	17%
Tree	8	4	8	1	8	6	10	3
Blackboard	29	69	18	78	44	47	28	72
Lion	26	5	29	1	11	3	10	0
Library	50	42	38	59	44	42	17	83
Rabbit	11	9	7	5	3	8	0	0
Painting	43	16	41	33	64	8	55	34
Boat	85	2	86	3	58	11	83	3
Book	38	52	24	75	47	36	28	72
Bird	10	12	7	7	11	8	0	0
Arithmetic page	36	60	26	72	53	31	34	66
Apple	18	12	17	25	11	19	24	14
School building	42	49	43	51	53	19	34	62
Alligator	25	4	22	1	14	6	14	0
Desk	40	51	34	61	56	19	31	69
Cup	32	57	30	62	22	58	41	45
Map	68	16	75	13	56	14	62	31
Carrot	7	3	8	11	11	11	3	3
Boy and girl at desk	37	56	21	77	67	19	24	69

Interpretation of these data is facilitated by assuming that the child's answers are determined primarily by his belief as to which sex is more frequently associated, in fantasy or reality, with the objects illustrated. This assumption is reasonable, for the young child prefers to define an object in terms of its functional relation to an agent, rather than in terms of the superordinate class to which it belongs. The fact that the majority of children labeled the rowboat masculine reflects the environmental contingency linking rowboats more frequently with men than with women. The face validity of this technique of assessing the child's symbolic classification of objects is supported by the child's responses to the nonschool pictures. All the children agreed that trees, rabbits, birds, apples, and carrots, as well as lion and alligator, were closer in meaning to farm than to masculine or feminine.

The labeling of the eight school-related objects that contained no cue as to gender (pencil, blackboard, library, book, arithmetic, school building, desk, and map) by the second graders indicated that more school objects were classified as feminine than masculine.[2] Two related statistical analyses were performed. In the first analysis, chi squares were computed for each item comparing the number of mas-

[2]Stimuli 7 and 19 (child painting and boy and girl at desk) were not included in this category. Additional observations revealed that the hand of the child painting resembled a boy's hand, and, therefore, was of dubious value. The S's answers confirmed this fact. The boy and girl at desk was intended as a control. It was expected that the boys would label it masculine and the girls would label it feminine. Except for the second-grade boys, this expectation was confirmed.

culine versus feminine answers for the whole group and for the sexes separately. It was assumed that the null hypothesis predicted an equal number of masculine and feminine labels to each item. This analysis revealed that blackboard, book, page of arithmetic, and school desk were each labeled feminine more frequently than masculine by the second-grade Ss ($p < .05$ or better for two tails). When this analysis was performed separately for the sexes, the differences were more pronounced for girls than for boys ($p < .01$ for each item for girls; $p < .01$ for page of arithmetic and blackboard for boys, but not significant for desk and book).

Since the proportion of feminine labels to these four items was greater than 50 per cent for both sexes, a second analysis asked whether the excess over 50 per cent was statistically significant.[3] These results were similar to those obtained with the first analysis. The differences were significant for girls for each of the four items ($p < .05$ or better). For boys, the differences were significant for arithmetic and blackboard ($p < .05$, $p < .01$), but were short of significance for desk and book.

Pencil and map were labeled masculine more frequently than feminine by both sexes ($p < .01$). The two remaining school-related items (library and school building) were not preferentially labeled masculine or feminine by the second-grade children. The masculine labeling of the map is probably due to the fact that the picture was a large map of the world, one that is often associated with astronauts, pilots, or navigators. Thus, this picture was linked with masculine vocations. The masculine labeling of the pencil is more puzzling. The post hoc interpretation that is offered is similar to that suggested for the map. The pencil illustrated was long, had an eraser, and resembled the type of pencil used by grocers and merchants—adults who are typically males.[4]

Data for the third-grade Ss are based on a smaller sample, and the conclusion should be regarded with greater caution. The data suggest that the older boys showed a slightly greater tendency to label the school items as masculine; whereas the older girls were more similar to the younger ones in maintaining the tendency to classify the school objects as predominantly feminine. More of the third-grade than second-grade boys called the four critical items masculine (blackboard, book, arithmetic, desk). Moreover, among third-grade boys, desk was more frequently labeled masculine than feminine ($p < .05$ by chi square analysis). The higher proportion of feminine to

---

[3]Using the formula $z = (P - .50) / \sqrt{pq / n}$ where p and $q = .50$.

[4]Many colleagues insist that the phallic form of the pencil was responsible for its masculine classification.

masculine labels among third-grade girls remained significant for blackboard, book, and desk ($p < .05$ by chi square), but missed significance for the page of arithmetic.

Finally, it may be of interest to note that the second graders were more likely to label the dangerous animals (lion, alligator) masculine than feminine ($p < .05$ for each). This result agrees with other work suggesting that young children are prone to classify males as more dangerous than females (Kagan et al., 1961). The decrease in this connotative association between dangerous objects and masculinity from grades 2 to 3 is the result of a stronger preference for linking lion or alligator with the concept farm than with masculinity.

Discussion

The results suggest that second-grade children view common objects in the classroom as more clearly associated with femininity than with masculinity. This finding should not be surprising. The child's definition of the sex-role characteristics of an object is derived from the differential frequency with which males and females are linked with the object. The typical primary school classroom is taught by a woman who works at the blackboard, passes out arithmetic, and teaches children to read books. As a result, the young child is persuaded to conceptualize these objects as more feminine than masculine. As the boy gains experience with social roles, he gradually learns that the acquisition of knowledge, reading, and mathematics are closely associated with masculine vocations, and the feminine classification of school objects should undergo some change. It is not unreasonable to argue that the disproportionate ratio of boys to girls with academic difficulties during the first four years of school is due, in part, to the young boy's categorization of school as a relatively feminine activity, and, therefore, not appropriate to his sex role. In sum, more young girls than boys view school activities as congruent with their sex role, and, consequently, they should be more highly motivated to master academic tasks.

There is one methodological implication of this study. The standard experimental strategy of concept transfer was used to determine the degree to which the child regarded school objects as masculine or feminine. An examiner cannot ask a child directly whether a pencil, a book, or a blackboard is male or female, for the child is likely to regard the question as nonsensical. But the disguise used in the transfer task appears to work. It is suggested that this paradigm of teaching the child a new label to represent a construct describing a motive, standard, or source of anxiety is potentially a powerful tool in the measurement of personality-related variables.

Caroline T. MacBrayer

Differences in Perception of the Opposite Sex by Males and Females

This selection indicates that both sexes tend to perceive males more favorably than females. Although MacBrayer's explanation, which is tied to the female's need for marriage, is distinctly of a social learning variety, her data support Freud's position equally well. Further studies by Sherriffs and Jarrett (1953), Fernberger (1948), and McKee and Sherriffs (1957) provide similar information about college students. The work of Tuddenham (1951, 1952) and of Smith (1939) illustrates that this tendency to devaluate females can be discerned even in school children in the early elementary grades. In this instance, of course, MacBrayer's "marriage-ability" explanation appears unlikely.

A. Problem

It has been experimentally established ". . . that the attitudes characteristic of different groups within a society tend to produce measurable differences in the perceptions and memories of the individuals who belong to them. Thus, whether a person is white or colored, rich or poor, Democrat or Republican, communist or anticommunist, religious or atheistic, tends in some measure to affect—to alter or even to distort—his perception and memory of objects and events in the world about him" (Crafts, Schneirla, Robinson, & Gilbert, 1950, p. 403). The present study is an investigation of differences in perception of the opposite sex by male and female college students as revealed by their completions of incomplete sentences relating to the opposite sex.

Formulation of specific hypotheses was somewhat limited by lack of experimentation in this area, but the general hypothesis was made that among young, unmarried adults, females perceive males more favorably than males perceive females. This hypothesis was based

Journal of Social Psychology, 1960, **52**, 309-314.

upon two assumptions. First, the androcentric bias (Zilboorg, 1944) was assumed to be operating among the college populations tested. The androcentric bias is ". . . the age-long theory of feminine inferiority proclaimed by man from time immemorial and seemingly accepted by the so-called really feminine women" (p. 262). Second, since value and need have been shown to magnify and enhance the perception of objects (Bruner & Goodman, 1947; Carter & Schooler, 1949), the assumption was made that in the United States, where spinsterhood is generally regarded as tantamount to failure, but bachelorhood carries no social stigma, marriageable females regard males as more valued and needed than marriageable males regard females.

B. Method

Subjects were 90 male college students in a small, denominational men's college and 125 female college students in a small women's college of the same denomination. *S*s were ignorant of the purpose of the experiment, key sentence completion items being embedded in what was presented by each of three instructors to their regular psychology classes as "a sentence completion test of personality." The four key items, as well as some of the "filler" items, were from the Sacks Sentence Completion Test (Sacks & Levy, 1952, pp. 377-378). The key items are given in Table 1.

Table 1.

Male subjects	Female subjects
1. I believe most women . . .	1. I believe most men . . .
2. I think most girls . . .	2. I think most boys . . .
3. My idea of a perfect woman . . .	3. My idea of a perfect man . . .
4. What I like least about women . . .	4. What I like least about men . . .

Each sentence completion was placed on a separate card and types of male and female completions were categorized for each of the four items. Four judges[1] collaborated on the formation of the categories. Using a miscellaneous category for the relatively few responses of a unique type, it was possible to categorize the completions for each sentence into 10 categories. The nature of the categories varied between items and, to a lesser extent, within items for the two sexes. It was found that rank-difference correlations between male and female responses could be calculated for the majority of the categories for Items 3 and 4.

[1]Appreciation is expressed to R. W. Gilbert, J. H. Reynolds, and W. T. Teachey, who assisted the author in formation of the categories.

C. Results

Results for males and females in terms of proportions of types of sentence completions for each of the four items are presented in Tables 2 through 5. Tables 2 and 3 reveal that college females perceive males more favorably than college males perceive females, the differences for both Items 1 and 2 being significant at better than the .01 level. For college males, proportions of favorable sentence comple-

Table 2. Proportions of Types of Sentence Completions by Males to "I Believe Most Women" and by Females to "I Believe Most Men"

Males			Females		
	Category			Category	
No.	Type of completion	p	No.	Type of completion	p
1.	Are beautiful or good	.22	1.	Are nice or intelligent	.42
2.	Seek marriage and its consequent		2.	Are ambitious	.17
	security	.18			
3.	Are inferior to men	.13	3.	Are interested in the opposite	
				sex	.12
4.	Are equal to men	.11	4.	Are normal	.07
5.	Are happiest as wives and mothers	.07	5.	Are immature or inconsiderate	.06
6.	Are self-centered	.07	6.	Are conceited	.05
7.	Are shallow or silly	.07	7.	Have high ideals	.04
8.	Talk too much or gossip	.06	8.	Are deceitful	.02
9.	Are extravagant	.02	9.	Are honest or fair	.02
10.	Miscellaneous	.07	10.	Miscellaneous	.03

Note.—Male Categories 1, 4, and 5 were classified as favorable, as were female Categories 1, 2, 3, 4, 7, and 9. All other categories were classified as unfavorable except No. 10, which was split evenly between unfavorable and favorable. The difference between proportions of favorable sentence completions for males ($p = .435$) and females ($p = .855$) was significant at better than the .01 level, z being 6.36.

Table 3. Proportions of Types of Sentence Completions by Males to "I Think Most Girls" and by Females to "I Think Most Boys"

Males			Females		
	Category			Category	
No.	Type of completion	p	No.	Type of completion	p
1.	Are nice company or good to have		1.	Are nice or wonderful	.50
	around	.34			
2.	Are shallow or silly	.20	2.	Are immature	.13
3.	Are marriage-minded	.12	3.	Are inconsiderate	.08
4.	Are mixed up or crazy	.08	4.	Are considerate	.07
5.	Are conceited	.06	5.	Are ambitious	.06
6.	Are attractive or sexy	.05	6.	Are conceited	.05
7.	Are less intelligent or able than		7.	Are alike or similar	.03
	men	.04			
8.	Are cold or indifferent	.02	8.	Like sports	.03
9.	Are sensible or honest	.02	9.	Are human beings	.02
10.	Miscellaneous	.07	10.	Miscellaneous	.03

Note.—Male Categories 1, 6, and 9 were classified as favorable, as were female Categories 1, 4, 5, 8, and 9. All other categories were classified as unfavorable except No. 10, which was split evenly between unfavorable and favorable. The difference between proportions of favorable sentence completions for males ($p = .445$) and females ($p = .695$) was significant at better than the .01 level, z being 3.57.

tions are strikingly similar for Item 1 (p = .435) and Item 2 (p = .445), which refer to women and girls, respectively. For college females, a larger proportion of favorable sentence completions was made for Item 1, which refers to men (p = .855) than for Item 2, which refers to boys (p = .695).

The most striking fact revealed by Tables 4 and 5 is the lack of agreement between males and females as to desirable and undesirable characteristics of the opposite sex. Rank-difference correlations between the seven categories which could be paired in Table 4 and the six categories which could be paired in Table 5 were insignificant (see Tables 4 and 5).

Table 4. Proportions of Types of Sentence Completions by Males to "My Idea of a Perfect Woman" and by Females to "My Idea of a Perfect Man"

	Males Category			Females Category	
No.	Type of completion	p	No.	Type of completion	p
1.	Is beautiful	.18	1.	Is considerate (4)	.29
2.	Is my girlfriend	.17	2.	Has a good character (6)	.26
3.	Doesn't exist	.17	3.	Is my boyfriend (2)	.18
4.	Is loving or understanding	.12	4.	Is mature or stable	.06
5.	Is intelligent	.10	5.	Is a family man or a good provider (7)	.06
6.	Has a good character	.09	6.	Is tall or handsome (1)	.05
7.	Is my mother or similar to my mother	.06	7.	Is intelligent (5)	.03
8.	Is congenial	.04	8.	Doesn't exist (3)	.02
9.	Is a certain movie star	.03	9.	Is rich	.02
10.	Miscellaneous	.04	10.	Miscellaneous	.03

Note.—Each number in parentheses following a female type of completion designates the number of the male category with which it was paired for calculation of a rank-difference coefficient of correlation, which is −.21.

Table 5. Proportions of Types of Sentence Completions by Males to "What I Like Least About Women" and by Females to "What I Like Least About Men"

	Males Category			Females Category	
No.	Type of completion	p	No.	Type of completion	p
1.	Deceitfulness or insincerity	.23	1.	Egoism or feeling of superiority (6)	.36
2.	Shallowness or silliness	.22	2.	Inconsiderateness (3)	.14
3.	Lack of dependability	.11	3.	Immaturity (2)	.13
4.	Talking too much	.10	4.	Crudeness or vulgarity (8)	.10
5.	Concern with appearance	.08	5.	Insincerity (1)	.10
6.	Self-centeredness	.06	6.	Stubbornness or sternness	.04
7.	Nothing to dislike	.06	7.	Aggressiveness	.03
8.	Use of foul language	.04	8.	Lack of understanding	.03
9.	Apathy or lack of ambition	.02	9.	Nothing comes to mind (7)	.03
10.	Miscellaneous	.08	10.	Miscellaneous	.04

Note.—Each number in parentheses following a female type of completion designates the number of the male category with which it was paired for calculation of a rank-difference coefficient of correlation, which is .07.

D. Discussion

Present results definitely confirm the hypothesis that among young, unmarried adults, females perceive males more favorably than males perceive females. This is probably due not only to androcentric bias (Zilboorg, 1944) on the part of males (and possibly some females), but also to enhancement of the female's perception of the male by the fact that he is relatively more needed and valued by her as a marriage partner. In the United States, marriage for women is both a security and a prestige goal, neither of which is ordinarily true for men. In fact, marriage for men usually involves assumption of financial responsibility and loss of cherished personal freedom. The male's feelings about marriage are to some extent reflected in the popular expressions which describe marriage as the "catching" or "trapping" of a man by a woman. The fact that sexual drive or need is stronger in the male than the female (Kinsey et al., 1948, 1953) might be expected to enhance the male's perception of the female more than the female's of the male. According to the present results, however, enhancement of the male's perception by this need is counteracted by androcentric bias and threat of marriage. Evidence that threat of marriage "de-enhances" the male's perception of the female is seen in Table 2, in which the completion "I think most women seek marriage and its consequent security" ranks second, and in Table 3, in which the completion "I think most girls are marriage-minded" ranks third.

The lack of correspondence between desirable and undesirable traits in the opposite sex reveals one source of tension and disagreement between the sexes. A difference in goals is shown in Table 4, where physical attractiveness ranks first for males and sixth for females, considerateness or understanding ranks first for females and fourth for males, and good character ranks second for females and sixth for males. Thus, sentence completions to Items 3 and 4 reveal a marked difference between male and female perceptions of desirable and undesirable traits in the opposite sex.

E. Summary

Four sentence completion items concerning the opposite sex were administered along with other incomplete sentences to 90 male and 125 female college students. Types of sentence completions for each of the four items were categorized for males and females and proportions of completions falling within each category determined. It was found that among young, unmarried adults, females perceive males significantly more favorably than males perceive females. This was interpreted as being due to androcentric bias, and to enhancement of the female's perception of the male by the fact that he is relatively more needed and valued by her as a marriage partner.

Philip Goldberg   Are Women Prejudiced against Women?

Although Goldberg's study deals only with female subjects, it illustrates the extensive nature of Mac-Brayer's findings and offers compelling support for an almost paradoxical deduction from Freudian theory: that females, as well as males, see women as inferior to men.

This is an unpleasant finding, and it raises a host of ethical questions that parallel those raised by the recent reawakening of the problem of black equality (see, for example, Coles, 1967). Although scientists strive to be objective and dispassionate in their search for knowledge, they cannot and perhaps should not rid themselves entirely of their commitments to value systems. Such commitments are reflected in the response of many members of the psychological community to the consistent evidence that blacks score lower than whites on most standard tests of intelligence. Many psychologists feel that this result indicates only that the tests are poorly designed; they argue that what we need now are either better tests, or equal opportunities to achieve on these tests, rather than continued collection of perhaps misleading and certainly damaging information.

A similar attitude toward data such as those reported by Goldberg, or toward the Freudian theory that they support, characterizes a large portion of the psychological (and nonpsychological) discipline. American society is marked by a strong commitment to equality—a commitment that is reflected in the choice of an infinitely malleable behaviorism as the dominant approach to psychological problems in this country. Theories that argue that individuals *are* certain ways because of hereditary, constitutional, or physiological properties that presumably cannot be changed may often be rejected on moral or ethical grounds, regardless of their elegance or the evidence supporting them.

Thus Goldberg's study, which confines itself to the data, carries implications that go far beyond those data and that force scientists—as well as the rest of us—to scrutinize those values that seem to us more important than the mere collection of data. The fact that both men and women accept female inferiority has been used, in one form or another, to justify the centuries of "double-standard" morality that have characterized Western civilization. And while we may think today that we have finally moved beyond that moral position, can we do so, Goldberg's study asks, if its foundations are still firmly entrenched in the belief systems of not only those who stand to gain by it (the men) but also of its victims?

Trans-action, 1968, **5** (May), 28-30. © 1968 by Trans-action Magazine, New Brunswick, N. J.

"Woman," advised Aristotle, "may be said to be an inferior man."

Because he was a man, Aristotle was probably biased. But what do women themselves think? Do they, consciously or unconsciously, consider their own sex inferior? And if so, does this belief prejudice them against other women—that is, make them view women, simply because they *are* women, as less competent than men?

According to a study conducted by myself and my associates, the answer to both questions is Yes. Women *do* consider their own sex inferior. And even when the facts give no support to this belief, they will persist in downgrading the competence—in particular, the intellectual and professional competence—of their fellow females.

Over the years, psychologists and psychiatrists have shown that both sexes consistently value men more highly than women. Characteristics considered male are usually praised; those considered female are usually criticized. In 1957 A.C. Sherriffs and J.P. McKee noted that "women are regarded as guilty of snobbery and irrational and unpleasant emotionality." Consistent with this report, E.G. French and G.S. Lesser found in 1964 that "women who value intellectual attainment feel they must reject the woman's role"—intellectual accomplishment apparently being considered, even among intellectual women, a masculine preserve. In addition, ardent feminists like Simone de Beauvoir and Betty Friedan believe that men, in important ways, are superior to women.

Now, is this belief simply prejudice, or are the characteristics and achievements of women really inferior to those of men? In answering this question, we need to draw some careful distinctions.

Different or Inferior?

Most important, we need to recognize that there are two distinct dimensions to the issue of sex differences. The first question is whether sex differences exist at all, apart from the obvious physical ones. The answer to this question seems to be a unanimous Yes— men, women, and social scientists agree that, psychologically and emotionally as well as physically, women *are* different from men.

But is being different the same as being inferior? It is quite possible to perceive a difference accurately but to value it inaccurately. Do women automatically view their differences from men as *deficiencies?* The evidence is that they do, and that this value judgment opens the door to anti-female prejudice. For if someone (male or female) concludes that women are inferior, his perceptions of women—their personalities, behavior, abilities, and accomplishments—will tend to be colored by his low expectations of women.

As Gordon W. Allport has pointed out in *The Nature of Prejudice,* whatever the facts about sex differences, anti-feminism—like any other prejudice—*distorts perception and experience*. What defines anti-feminism is not so much believing that women are inferior, as allowing that belief to distort one's perceptions of women. More generally, it is not the partiality itself, but the distortion born of that partiality, that defines prejudice.

Thus, an anti-Semite watching a Jew may see devious or sneaky behavior. But, in a Christian, he would regard such behavior only as quiet, reserved, or perhaps even shy. Prejudice is self-sustaining: It continually distorts the "evidence" on which the prejudiced person claims to base his beliefs. Allport makes it clear that anti-feminism, like anti-Semitism or any other prejudice, consistently twists the "evidence" of experience. We see not what is there, but what we *expect* to see.

The purpose of our study was to investigate whether there is real prejudice by women against women—whether perception itself is distorted unfavorably. Specifically, will women evaluate a professional article with a jaundiced eye when they think it is the work of a woman, but praise the same article when they think its author is a man? Our hypotheses were:

Even when the work is identical, women value the professional work of men more highly than that of women.

But when the professional field happens to be one traditionally reserved for women (nursing, dietetics), this tendency will be reversed, or at least greatly diminished.

Some 140 college girls, selected at random, were our subjects. One hundred were used for the preliminary work; 40 participated in the experiment proper.

To test the second hypothesis, we gave the 100 girls a list of 50 occupations and asked them to rate "the degree to which you associate the field with men or with women." We found that law and city planning were fields strongly associated with men, elementary-school teaching and dietetics were fields strongly associated with women, and two fields—linguistics and art history—were chosen as neutrals, not strongly associated with either sex.

Now we were ready for the main experiment. From the professional literature of each of these six fields, we took one article. The articles were edited and abridged to about 1500 words, then combined into two equal sets of booklets. The crucial manipulation had to do with the authors' names—the same article bore a male name in one set of booklets, a female name in the other set. An example: If, in set one, the first article bore the name John T. McKay, in set two the same article would appear under the name Joan T. McKay. Each booklet contained three articles by "men" and three articles by "women."

The girls, seated together in a large lecture hall, were told to read the articles in their booklets and given these instructions:

> In this booklet you will find excerpts of six articles, written by six different authors in six different professional fields. At the end of each article you will find several questions. . . . You are not presumed to be sophisticated or knowledgeable in all the fields. We are interested in the ability of college students to make critical evaluations. . . .

Note that no mention at all was made of the authors' sexes. That information was contained—apparently only by coincidence—in the author's names. The girls could not know, therefore, what we were really looking for.

At the end of each article were nine questions asking the girls to rate the articles for value, persuasiveness, and profundity—and to rate the authors for writing style, professional competence, professional status, and ability to sway the reader. On each item, the girls gave a rating of from 1 (highly favorable) to 5 (highly unfavorable).

Generally, the results were in line with our expectations—but not completely. In analyzing these results, we used three different methods: We compared the amount of anti-female bias in the different occupational fields (would men be rated as better city planners, but women as better dieticians?); we compared the amount of bias shown on the nine questions that followed each article (would men be rated as more competent, but women as more persuasive?); and we ran an overall comparison, including both fields and rating questions.

Starting with the analysis of bias by occupational field, we immediately ran into a major surprise. (See table on p. 66.) That there is a general bias by women against women, and that it is strongest in traditionally masculine fields, was clearly borne out. But in other fields the situation seemed rather confused. We had expected the anti-female trend to be reversed in traditionally feminine fields. But it appears that, even here, women consider themselves inferior to men. Women seem to think that men are better at *everything*—including elementary-school teaching and dietetics!

Scrutiny of the nine rating questions yielded similar results. On all nine questions, regardless of the author's occupational field, the girls consistently found an article more valuable—and its author more competent—when the article bore a male name. Though the articles themselves were exactly the same, the girls felt that those written by the John T. McKays were definitely more impressive, and reflected more glory on their authors, than did the mediocre offerings of the Joan T. McKays. Perhaps because the world has accepted female

Law: A Strong Masculine Preserve

Field of Article	Mean	
	Male	Female
Art history	23.35	23.10
Dietetics	22.05	23.45
Education	20.20	21.75
City planning	23.10	27.30
Linguistics	26.95	30.70
Law	21.20	25.60

These are the total scores the college girls gave to the six pairs of articles they read. The lowest possible score—9—would be the most favorable; the highest possible score—54—the most critical. While male authors received more favorable ratings in all occupational fields, the differences were statistically significant only in city planning, linguistics, and—especially—law.

authors for a long time, the girls were willing to concede that the female professionals' writing styles were not *far* inferior to those of the men. But such a concession to female competence was rare indeed.

Statistical analysis confirms these impressions and makes them more definite. With a total of six articles, and with nine questions after each one, there were 54 points at which comparisons could be drawn between the male authors and the female authors. Out of these 54 comparisons, three were tied, seven favored the female authors—and the number favoring the male authors was 44!

Clearly, there is a tendency among women to downgrade the work of professionals of their own sex. But the hypothesis that this tendency would decrease as the "femaleness" of the professional field increased was not supported. Even in traditionally female fields, anti-feminism holds sway.

Since the articles supposedly written by men were exactly the same as those supposedly written by women, the perception that the men's articles were superior was obviously a distortion. For reasons of their own, the female subjects were sensitive to the sex of the author, and this apparently irrelevant information biased their judgments. Both the distortion and the sensitivity that precedes it are characteristic of prejudice. Women—at least these young college women—are prejudiced against female professionals and, regardless of the actual accomplishments of these professionals, will firmly refuse to recognize them as the equals of their male colleagues.

Is the intellectual double-standard really dead? Not at all—and if the college girls in this study are typical of the educated and presumably progressive segments of the population, it may not even be dying. Whatever lip service these girls pay to modern ideas of equality between men and women, their beliefs are staunchly traditional. Their real coach in the battle of the sexes is not Simone de Beauvoir or Betty Friedan. Their coach is Aristotle.

Two

Intrapersonal and Interpersonal Behavior

As the heading suggests, the readings in this section could discuss almost the entire range of behaviors, thoughts, and feelings that are usually considered under "Personality." Obviously, some restrictions must be made.

One such restriction is the omission of studies dealing with the *development* of sex differences in favor of studies describing and defining already well-formed character tendencies in adulthood or adolescence. (An excellent, up-to-date summary of the development of sex differences can be found in Maccoby (1966)—particularly in Oetzel's chapter in that book.)

As a further restriction, I have chosen readings for this section that deal with some of the less obvious areas of sex differences. For example, we will find pronounced sex differences in dreams (the readings by Hall and Paolino), in the use of toys to construct imaginary scenes (Erikson), and in ability to memorize names and faces (Kaess and Witryol). Indeed, it sometimes appears that, if there is any area of human behavior in which sex differences have *not* been discovered, it is only because no one has yet designed a study to tap that area.

However, although it may be possible to prove the *existence* of sex differences in most areas, it is not easy to assess their *importance*. At least two of the readings in this section (that by Schaeffer and Eisenberg, dealing with noncompetitive conflict, and that by Singer and Stefflre, dealing with job aspirations) suggest that the sex differences found in their studies were far less significant than might have been predicted. (The selection by Spiegel, Brodkin, and Keith-Spiegel in Part Three makes the same point.)

Unfortunately, the whole question of trying to estimate the *importance* of a given variable (such as sex) is extraordinarily difficult for a variety of reasons. First, such importance can only be assessed with regard to some criterion. For example, sex differences are presumably very significant when one is applying for a job as a Playboy Bunny but almost negligible when one is learning to swim. Second, even with a fixed criterion in mind—say, applying for a job as a Playboy Bunny—the importance of sex differences can be assessed only relative to the *importance* of some other factor, such as age, race, or attractiveness. Third, the relative importance of the differences will fluctuate according to the particular *situation* in which they are being assessed. That is, if Playboy opened a club in Antarctica, the scarcity of females to serve as Bunnies in that region might make the distinction somewhat less important than it is in New York City. Obviously, then, the word *important* is very slippery; it is at best relative, and it is specific to situations.

Erik H. Erikson   Sex Differences
                         in the Play
                         Configurations of
                         Preadolescents
                         (Excerpt)

This section was one of Erikson's first contributions to attract wide attention among personality and developmental psychologists. It precedes by some years his better-known work dealing with the eight stages of development and, particularly, problems of identity. Nevertheless, the reading excerpted here shows all the qualities found in his later studies—his extremely lucid and compelling literary style, the warm humanism to which it is harnessed, and, all too often, his lesser concern for the rigors of statistical analysis than for brilliant clinical intuition.

I should say a few words about this question of statistical rigor, which has already come up with regard to Blum's selection (p. 22) and will continue to pose difficulties later in this text. The essence of the problem is that, although science generally strives for the *understanding* of natural phenomena, such understanding is only possible (among scientists, at any rate) when it is based on a foundation of fairly general *laws* or principles. In psychology these principles can only be established by means of statistical analyses; thus, for the present time at least, our psychology can only be as good as our statistical foundations.

Yet statistical elegance has only been fashionable and possible in psychology since the mid-1950s—well after Erikson made this study. Consequently, one cannot demand too much of his contribution on that ground. On the other hand, the increased sophistication of our knowledge of statistical methods today allows us to look at Erikson's (and similar) works more searchingly now than when they appeared. I suggest that the reader consider the following points while reading this selection:

First, Erikson's analysis was one of two that dealt with the same experiment. The other, by Honzik (1951), was concerned with differences between the sexes in *choice* of materials for play constructions, rather than with the way these materials were used. Thus Honzik's study is on far safer grounds statistically.

Second, Erikson's study dealt with two groups of children, a "clinic" group referred for counseling and a normal "control" group. The children were all seen and tested at roughly half-year intervals for three or more years. Thus the children in his 11- and 12- and 13-year-old groups were all more or less the same individuals at different ages. However, Erikson did not seem to be

Excerpted from the *American Journal of Orthopsychiatry*, 1951, **21**, 667-692. This selection originally appeared on pages 681-692; three figures have been omitted.

aware of the problems this method posed and did not feel any need, for example, to discuss the difference between children at age 11, when the girls built many more enclosures than the boys, and the same children at age 13, when the boys built far more such enclosures.

Third, early in this excerpt Erikson points to four "significant" sex differences in the use of enclosures. Of these, the first reaches statistical significance only for one age group, the second never reaches the customary .05 level of statistical significance, and no data are presented in support of the third or fourth. Moreover, interpretation of Erikson's data is complicated by an occasional misprint in his tables. For example, in Table 2 the entry for 11-year-olds in the "Enclosing" row clearly *cannot* be a critical ratio of +3.3; if the associated percentages

(17% and 41%) are correct—and they appear to be—this value should be − 3.3.

Finally, because Erikson's classification of the various constructions appears to have been determined largely on a post hoc basis, it may be questioned whether he was not setting up these categories in a manner that "stacked the cards" in favor of his hypotheses. There is nothing wrong with this methodology if one is doing exploratory work, but results discerned in this manner should be confirmed by replication on an independent sample.

Nevertheless, these criticisms do not seriously affect the meaning of Erikson's conclusions. What he may lack in mathematical elegance is more than compensated for by the acuity and lucidity of his clinical insights.

. . . The most significant sex differences, then, concern the tendency among the boys to erect structures, buildings and towers, or to build streets; among the girls, to take the play table to be the interior of a house, with simple, little, or no use of blocks (see Table 1).

The configurational approach to the matter can be made more specific by showing the spatial function emphasized in the various ways of using (or not using) blocks. This organization would combine all the constructions which share the function of *channelizing* traffic (such as lanes, tunnels or crossings); all elaborate buildings and special structures (such as bridges, boats, etc.) which owe their character to the tendency of *erecting* and *constructing;* all simple walls, which merely *enclose* interiors; and all house interiors, which are without benefit of enclosing walls and are thus simply *open interiors*. These sex differences are shown in Table 2.

In the special case of the *enclosures*, it was necessary to add the differentiation of "in conjunction" or "not in conjunction" with other configurations in order to verify the clinical impression that the preferential or exclusive manifestation of a simple enclosing tendency is generally feminine. To build a rectangular arrangement of simple walls is about the most common way of indicating "a house" and, therefore, not apt to express any particular differentiation. But it was

Intrapersonal and Interpersonal Behavior

Table 1. Significance of the Sex Differences in the Form of the Play Configurations.

	11 Years Boys N=79 %	11 Years Girls N=78 %	11 Years Diff. / SE Diff.	12 Years Boys N=80 %	12 Years Girls N=81 %	12 Years Diff. / SE Diff.	13 Years Boys N=77 %	13 Years Girls N=73 %	13 Years Diff. / SE Diff.
I. Block Configuration									
A. Sidewalk	2	2		3	4		3	1	
B. Freestanding wall	7	4		4	2		6	6	
C. Lane	12	4	1.86	13	4	2.05*	6	3	
D. Tunnel	3	—		1	—		—	—	
E. Crossing	2			—	—		3	1	
F. Partitions	10	11		11	9		8	6	
G. Enclosure	27	41	1.86	38	33		39	27	
H. Building	22	14	1.31	31	7	4.06†	25	10	1.57
J. Tower	9	3		11	3	2.01*	12	1	2.49*
K. Miscellaneous structures	22	12	1.67	13	15		15	14	2.83†
L. Ruin	4	—		3	2		5	3	
II. Configuration of Furniture									
A. One room	14	24	1.62	6	19	2.52†	4	23	3.54†
B. Two rooms	1	8		3	11	2.01*	1	4	
III. Configuration of Animals	6	6		3	11	2.01*	1	8	
IV. Configuration of Cars	21	11	1.73	15	15		23	14	1.42

* Significant at the 5% level.
† Significant at the 1% level.

Table 2. Significance of the Sex Differences in the Spatial Functions of the Play Configurations.

| | 11 Years | | | | 12 Years | | | | 13 Years | | | |
	Boys N=79 %	Girls N=78 %	Diff.	SE Diff.	Boys N=80 %	Girls N=81 %	Diff.	SE Diff.	Boys N=77 %	Girls N=73 %	Diff.	SE Diff.
Channelizing	17	4	+2.7†		13.6	4	+2.2*		9	3.7	+1.3	
Erecting	53	29	+3.1†		55	25	+3.9†		52	25	+3.4†	
Enclosing	17	41	+3.3†		38	33	+.7		39	27	+1.6	
In conjunction	15	14	+.2		25	14	+1.7		26	6	+3.3†	
Not in conjunction with other configurations	7	14	-1.4		10	14	-.8		7	14	-1.4	
Interiors	14.6	32	-2.6†		9	30	-3.4†		5	27	-3.7†	

* Significant at the 5% level.
† Significant at the 1% level.

found that, in the case of many boys, simple enclosures in the form of front yards and back yards were only added to more elaborate buildings; or that simple corrals or barnyards would appear in connection with outdoor scenes. In this category, therefore, only more detailed work showed that (1) significantly more boys than girls build enclosures only in conjunction with elaborate structures or traffic lanes; (2) significantly more girls than boys will be satisfied with the exclusive representation of a simple enclosure; (3) girls *include* a significantly greater number of (static) objects and people within their enclosures; (4) boys *surround* their enclosures with a significantly greater number of (moving) objects.

Height of structure, then, is prevalent in the configurations of the boys. The observation of the unique details which accompany constructions of extreme height suggests that the variable representing the opposite of elevation, i.e., *downfall*, is equally typical for boys. Fallen-down structures, namely, "ruins," are exclusively found in boys,[1] a fact which did not change in the days of the war when girls as well as boys must have been shocked by pictorial reports of destroyed homes. In connection with the very highest towers, something in the nature of a downward trend appears regularly, but in such a diverse form that only individual examples can illustrate what is meant: one boy, after much indecision, took his extraordinarily high tower down in order to build a final configuration of a simple and low character; another balanced his tower very precariously and pointed out that the immediate danger of collapse was in itself the exciting factor in his story, in fact, *was* his story. In two cases extremely high and well-built facades with towers were incongruously combined with low irregular enclosures. One boy who built an especially high tower put a prone boy doll at the foot of it and explained that this boy had fallen down from its height; another boy left the boy doll sitting high on one of several elaborate towers but said that the boy had had a mental breakdown and that the tower was an insane asylum. The very highest tower was built by the very smallest boy; and, to climax lowness, a colored boy built his structure *under* the table. In these and similar ways, variations of a theme make it apparent that *the variable high-low* is a *masculine variable*. To this generality, we would add the clinical judgment that, in preadolescent boys, extreme height (in its regular combination with an element of breakdown or fall) reflects a trend

---

[1] One single girl built a ruin. This girl, who suffered from a fatal blood disease, at the time was supposed to be unaware of the fact that only a new medical procedure, then in its experimental stages, was keeping her alive. Her story presented the mythological theme of a "girl who miraculously returned to life after having been sacrificed to the gods." She has since died.

toward the emotional overcompensation of a doubt in or a fear for one's masculinity, while varieties of "lowness" express passivity and depression.

Girls rarely build towers. When they do, they seem unable to make them stand freely in space. Their towers lean against or stay close to the background. The highest tower built by any girl was not on the table at all, but on a shelf in a niche in the wall beside and behind the table. The clinical impression is that, in girls of this age, the presence of a tower connotes the masculine overcompensation of an ambivalent dependency on the mother, which is indicated in the closeness of the structure to the background. There are strong clinical indications that a scene's "clinging" to the background connotes "mother fixation," while the extreme foreground serves to express counterphobic overcompensation.

In addition to the dimensions "high" and "low," and "forward" and "backward," "open" and "closed" suggest themselves as significant. As the tables indicate, open interiors of houses are built by a majority of girls. In many cases this interior is expressly peaceful. Where it is a home rather than a school, somebody, usually a little girl, plays the piano: a remarkably tame "exciting movie scene" for representative preadolescent girls. In a number of cases, however, a disturbance occurs. An intruding pig throws the family in an uproar and forces the girl to hide behind the piano; the father may, to the family's astonishment, be coming home riding on a lion; a teacher has jumped on a desk because a tiger has entered the room. This intruding element is always a man, a boy, or an animal. If it is a dog, it is always expressly a boy's dog. Disturbed and endangered are either the whole family with a majority of women and girls or women and girls exclusively. Strangely enough, in girls, this idea of an intruding creature does not lead to the defensive erection of walls or to the closing of doors. Rather, the majority of these intrusions have an element of humor and of pleasurable excitement and occur in connection with open interiors consisting of circular arrangements of furniture.

To indicate the way in which such regularities became apparent through exceptions to the rule, we wish to report briefly how three of these "intrusive" configurations came to be built by boys. Two were built by the same boy in two successive years. Each time a single male figure, surrounded by a circle of furniture, was intruded upon by wild animals. This boy at the time was obese, of markedly feminine build, and, in fact, under thyroid treatment. Shortly after this treatment had taken effect, the boy became markedly masculine. In his third construction he built one of the highest and slenderest of all towers. Oth-

erwise, there was only one other boy who, in a preliminary construction, had a number of animals intrude into an "open interior" which
contained a whole family. When already at the door, he suddenly
turned back, exclaimed that "something was wrong," and with an
expression of satisfaction, rearranged the animals along a tangent
which led them close by but away from the family circle.

Enclosures are the largest item among the configurations built
by girls, if, as pointed out, we consider primarily those enclosures
which include a house interior. These enclosures often have a richly
ornamented gate (the only configuration which girls care to elaborate in detail); in others, openness is counteracted by a blocking of
the entrance or a thickening of the walls. The general clinical impression here is that high and thick walls reflect either acute anxiety over
the feminine role, or, in conjunction with other configurations, acute
oversensitiveness and self-centeredness. The significantly larger number of open interiors and simple enclosures, combined with an emphasis, in unique details, on intrusion into the interiors; on an exclusive
elaboration of doorways; and the blocking off of such doorways
seems to mark *open and closed* as a feminine variable.

Interpretation of Results

The most significant sex differences in the use of the play space,
then, add up to the following picture: in the boys, the outstanding
variables are height and downfall, and motion and its channelization
or arrest (policeman); in girls, static interiors, which are open, simply
enclosed, or blocked and intruded upon.

In the case of boys, these configurational tendencies are connected
with a generally greater emphasis on the outdoors and the outside,
and in girls, with an emphasis on house interiors.

The selection of the subjects of the Guidance Study assures the fact
that the boys and girls who built these constructions are as masculine
and feminine as they come in a representative group in our
community. We may, therefore, assume that these sex differences are
a representative expression of masculinity and of femininity for this
particular age group. In the interpretation of these data, questions
arise which are based on the dichotomy between biological motivation
and cultural motivation, and on that between conscious and unconscious sexual attitudes.

The exclusively cultural interpretation would grow out of the
assumption that these children emphasize in their constructions the
sex roles defined for them by their particular cultural setting. In this
case, the particular use of blocks would be a logical function of the

manifest content of the themes presented. Thus, if boys concentrate on the exterior of buildings, on bridges and traffic lanes, the conclusion would be that this is a result of their actual or anticipated experience, which takes place outdoors more than does that of girls, and that they anticipate construction work and travel while the girls themselves know that their place is supposed to be in the home. A boy's tendency to picture outward and upward movement may, then, be only another expression of a general sense of obligation to prove himself strong and aggressive, mobile and independent in the world, and to achieve, as it were, high standing. As for the girls, their representation of house interiors (which has such a clear antecedent in their infantile play with toys) would then mean that they are concentrating on the anticipated task of taking care of a home and of rearing children, either because their upbringing has made them want to do this or because they think they are supposed to indicate that they want to do this.

A glance at the selection of elements and themes in their relation to conscious sex roles demonstrates how many questions remain unanswered if a one-sided cultural explanation is accepted as the sole basis for the sex differences expressed in these configurations.

If the boys, in building these scenes, think primarily of their present or anticipated roles, why are not boy dolls the figures most frequently used by them? The policeman is their favorite; yet it is safe to say that few anticipate being policemen, or believe that they should. Why do the boys not arrange any sport fields in their play constructions? With the inventiveness born of strong motivation, this could have been accomplished, as could be seen in the construction of one football field, with grandstand and all. But this was arranged by a girl who at the time was obese and tomboyish, and wore "affectedly short-trimmed hair"—all of which suggests a unique determination in her case.

As mentioned before, during the early stages of the Study, World War II approached and broke out; to be an aviator became one of the most intense hopes of many boys. Yet the pilot shows preferred treatment in both boys and girls only over the monk, and—over the baby. The policeman, most frequently used by boys, occurs in their constructions twice as often as the cowboy, who certainly is the more immediate role-ideal of these Western boys and most in keeping with the clothes they wear and the attitudes they affect.

If the girls' prime motivation is the love of their present homes and the anticipation of their future ones to the exclusion of all aspirations which they might be sharing with boys, it still would not immediately explain why the girls build fewer and lower walls around their houses. Love for home life would justify rather an increase in high walls and closed doors as guarantors of intimacy and security. The majority of the girl dolls in these peaceful family scenes are playing the piano or peacefully sitting with their families in the living room: could this be really considered representative of what they want to do or think they should pretend they want to do when asked to build an exciting movie scene?

A piano-playing little girl, then, seems as specific for the representation of a peaceful interior in the girls' constructions as traffic arrested by the policeman is for the boys' street scenes. The first can be understood to express *goodness indoors;* the second, a guarantor of safety and *caution outdoors*. Such emphasis on goodness and safety, in response to the explicit instruction to construct an "exciting movie scene," suggests that in these preadolescent scenes dynamic dimensions are involved which go deeper than a theory of mere compliance with cultural and conscious ideals would have it; the other projective methods used in the study do not seem to call forth such desire to depict virtue.

The questions mentioned point to the caution necessary in settling on any one dichotomized view concerning the motivations leading to the sex differences in these constructions. It is with such caution that we, finally, turn to the indication of clearly biological determinants in the play constructions. The dominant trends outlined call to mind the dominant trends in the play constructions of college students in an exploratory study. There the tendency was, among men, to emphasize (by dramatization or avoidance) potential disaster to women. Most commonly, a little girl was run over by a truck. But while this item occurred in practically all cases in the preliminary and abortive constructions, it remained a central theme in fewer of the final constructions. In the women's constructions, the theme of an insane or criminal man was universal: he broke into the house at night, or at any rate, was where he should not be. At the time we had no alternative but to conclude tentatively that what these otherwise highly individual play scenes had in common was an expression of the sexual frustration adherent to the age and the mores of these college students. These young men and women, so close to complete intimacy with the other sex and shying away only from its last technical consummation, were dramatizing in their constructions (among other latent themes) fantasies of sexual violence which would override prohibition and inhibition.

Our group of children, developmentally speaking, stand at the beginning of sexual maturation, and it may well be that this, among other things, is expressed in their constructions. For it is clear that the spatial tendencies governing these constructions closely parallel the morphology of the sex organs: in the male, *external* organs, *erectible* and *intrusive* in character, serving highly *mobile* sperm cells; *internal* organs in the female, with vestibular *access*, leading to *statically expectant* ova.

Only comparative material, derived from older and younger subjects living through other developmental periods, can answer the question whether our data reflect an acute and temporary emphasis on the modalities of the sexual organs owing to the experience of oncoming sexual maturation, or whether our data suggest that the two sexes may live, as it were, in time-spaces of a different quality, in basically different fields of "means-end-readiness" (Tolman, 1932). How early spatial expression may thus be differentiated, and to which areas of experience, action and thought such differentiation may extend are problems of research suggested by our study.[2]

The configurational approach, then, provides an anchor for interpretation in the ground plan of the human body: here, sex difference obviously provides the most significant over-all differentiation. In the interplay of thematic content and spatial configuration, then, we come to recognize an expression of that interpenetration of the biological, cultural and psychological, which, in psychoanalysis, we have learned to summarize as the *psychosexual*.

Cultures, after all, elaborate upon the biologically given and at least attempt to arrive at a division of labor between the sexes, which is, simultaneously, workable within the body's scheme and life cycle, useful to the particular culture, and manageable for the individual ego.

In conclusion, a word on the house as a symbol and as a subject of metaphors. While the spatial tendencies related here extend to three-dimensionality as such, the construction of a house by the use of simple, standardized blocks obviously serves to make the matter more concrete and more measurable. Not only in regard to the representation of sex differences but also in connection with the hypochondriac preoccupation with other growing or afflicted body parts, we have learned to assume an unconscious tendency to represent the body and its parts in terms of a building and its parts. And, indeed, Freud said

---

[2]In a not yet completed study, Dr. Kenneth Colby surveyed the first dreams reported in the published case histories of 100 men and 100 women patients from Western Europe and the United States. He tentatively reports, for men, a preponderance of sudden and fast-moving events; of vehicle traffic, especially train engines; of guns and machines; of hitting out; of authorities and of being pursued by police; and of being ineffectual and paralyzed. In women, he finds a comparative preponderance of stationary situations; of houses, doors, windows; of clothes; of food; of children, babies, dogs and birds; of being compelled and encroached upon.

For an application of the configurational trends indicated here in a Masculinity-Femininity test, see Franck (1946).

fifty years ago, "The only typical, that is to say, regularly occurring representation of the human form as a whole is that of a house" (1922).

We use this metaphor consciously too. We speak of our body's "build"; and of the "body" of vessels, carriages and churches. In spiritual and poetic analogies, the body carries the connotation of an abode, prison, refuge, or temple inhabited by, well, ourselves: "This mortal house," as Shakespeare put it. Such metaphors, with varying abstractness and condensation, express groups of ideas which are sometimes too high, sometimes too low, for words. In slang, too, every outstanding part of the body, beginning with the "underpinnings," appears translated into metaphors of house parts. Thus, the face is a "façade," the eyes "front windows with shutters," the mouth a "barn door" with a "picket fence," the throat a "drain pipe," the chest a "bone house" (which is also a term used for the whole body), the male genital is referred to as a "water pipe," and the rectum as the "sewer." Whatever this proves, it does show that it takes neither erudition nor a special flair for symbolism to understand these metaphors. Yet, for some of us, it is easier to take such symbolism for granted on the stage of drama and burlesque than in dreams or in children's play; in other words, it is easier to accept such representation when it is lifted to sublime or lowered to laughable levels.

The further study of the interrelation of verbal, thematic and spatial expression in play may help to cut through the semantic connotations and conventional clichés which cloud the issue of sex differences and of psychosexual differentiation. The gain from such studies for the psychology of space will be discussed elsewhere.

Calvin Hall

A Modest Confirmation of Freud's Theory of a Distinction between the Superego of Men and Women

Hall's brief selection on aggression and misfortune in the dreams of males and females is a model of the felicitous interplay of theory and data. In essence, Hall has pared Freudian theory down to simple, individual hypotheses, applied each one in a direct and straightforward manner to the large mass of data he had available, and produced clear proof or refutation of each one in turn. As he has remarked elsewhere (Hall, 1963), "When a theory tells us what we will find if we look in a certain place—and we look there and we do find what has been predicted —then the theory has done its work well."

Hall's works stem from analysis of the more than 30,000 dreams he has collected at his Institute for Dream Research. The reading reprinted here is only one of a series of brief gems that he has produced in the past several years. Others in this series have offered confirmation of the Oedipus complex (Hall, 1963), sex differences in aggression (Hall & Domhoff, 1963), and castration anxiety (Hall & Van de Castle, 1965).

Freud observed that a woman's superego is "never so inexorable, so impersonal, so independent of its emotional origins as we require it to be in men." In other words, the female superego is not as fully internalized as that of the male. Two testable hypotheses were derived from this theory. It was hypothesized that in their dreams (a) women would be more often the victim of aggression and (b) men would more often suffer a misfortune. The data for the study were obtained from the content analysis of 3,049 dreams. Both hypotheses were confirmed.

Journal of Abnormal and Social Psychology, 1964, **69**, 440-442. © 1964 by the American Psychological Association and reproduced by permission. Research supported in part by Grant M-6475(A) from the National Institute of Mental Health, United States Public Health Service.

He accounts for this difference in male and female superego in terms of Oedipal theory.

Under the influence of the danger of losing his penis, he [the boy] abandons his Oedipus-complex; it is repressed and in the most normal cases entirely destroyed, while a severe super-ego is set up as its heir. What happens in the case of the girl is almost the opposite. The castration-complex prepares the way for the Oedipus-complex instead of destroying it.... The girl remains in the Oedipus situation for an indefinite period, she only abandons it late in life, and then incompletely. The formation of the super-ego must suffer in these circumstances; it cannot attain the strength and independence which gives it its cultural importance... (Freud, 1933, pp. 176-177).

In other words, the distinction that Freud made between the male and the female superego is one of a more or less internalized superego. The less internalized superego is still dependent to some extent upon its sources in the external world. These sources are, in Freudian theory, the punishing and rewarding parents, or their surrogates. The fully internalized superego is one which has become independent of these parental sources. A person whose superego development is retarded so that it remains externalized tends to disown his guilt and to fear and to blame external enemies. A person whose superego development has attained a full measure of incorporation in the personality acknowledges his own guilt and blames himself. For such a person the critical agent is his own conscience.

We think it is this distinction between *internalized* and *externalized* (the distinction is relative and not absolute) that Freud had in mind when he described the female superego as less inexorable, more personal, and more dependent on its emotional origin than the superego of the male. The conscience of the woman is less inexorable because one can more easily evade an external authority than escape from an internalized conscience; more personal because the punitive agents are personified individuals rather than inner, impersonal feelings; and more dependent upon its emotional origins because the battle waged by an externalized superego is against the emotionally charged parental figures of early childhood.

Only a fully internalized superego can be of cultural importance because the stability of society depends more upon directives from the voice of conscience than from the sanctions and prohibitions of external authority.

So much then for the theory upon which this investigation is based. From the theory as stated, we have derived several propositions which can be tested on data secured from dreams. In order to make these propositions comprehensible it is necessary to present some introductory considerations.

Among the manuals which we have prepared for making content analyses of reported dreams is one for classifying aggressions and misfortunes in dreams (Institute of Dream Research, 1962). In the analysis of aggression, a distinction is made between those aggressive encounters in which the dreamer is the aggressor and those in which he is the victim of intentional aggression from another character or characters in the dream. A third class of aggressive interactions in which there is no clearly defined aggressor or victim does not figure in the present investigation. In the analysis of misfortunes (which exclude, of course, any misfortune in connection with an aggressive encounter), a distinction is made between misfortunes to the dreamer and misfortune to other characters in the dream. A misfortune does not involve any social interaction, at least, of an intentional, premeditated, or motivated sort. A victim of misfortune is a victim of circumstance, accident, or of his own incapacities. Misfortunes include such items as illness, injury, adversity, loss or destruction of property, frustration, delay, encountering an obstacle, inability to do something, failure, and being lost.

The hypotheses to be tested in this investigation rest upon two assumptions. First, it is assumed that dreams in which the dreamer is the victim of aggression are expressions of an externalized superego. Second, it is assumed that dreams in which the dreamer is the victim of misfortune are expressions of an internalized superego.

Now we can state the hypotheses in data-oriented terms.

1. In female dreams, there will be a higher proportion of dreams in which the dreamer is the victim of aggression than in male dreams.

2. In male dreams, there will be a higher proportion of dreams in which the dreamer suffers a misfortune than in female dreams.

The data for this study were obtained from the analysis of more than 3,000 dreams which were collected primarily from young adults. They were written down by the dreamer on a standard report form which the writer has used for a number of years in collecting dreams.

The results are presented in Tables 1 and 2. The difference between the two proportions in Table 1 is significant at less than the .01 level.

Table 1. Proportion of Aggressions in Which the Dreamer Is the Victim.

	Dreams	
	Male	*Female*
Number of dreams	1,494	1,555
Number of aggressions	534	492
Proportion of aggressions in which the dreamer is the victim	.58	.68

Table 2. *Proportion of Misfortunes Which Happen to the Dreamer.*

	Dreams	
	Male	*Female*
Number of dreams	1,494	1,555
Number of misfortunes	410	397
Proportion of misfortunes to the dreamer	.65	.49

Both hypotheses are confirmed. Consequently, it is concluded that evidence from aggression and misfortune dreams supports Freud's view that the superego of the female is less internalized than is the superego of the male. This confirmation is considered to be a modest one because it involves only two hypotheses and because the data are derived from one type of material, namely, reported dreams. Complete confirmation of Freud's theory of the differences between the male superego and the female superego requires the testing of a number of hypotheses in a variety of situations with different populations.

Albert F. Paolino

Dreams: Sex Differences in Aggressive Content

Paolino's content analysis of the dreams of his subjects represents one of the fairly rare examples (besides the studies of Calvin Hall) of the use of this material for primarily statistical analyses of groups. Since the time of Freud, of course, dreams have been a rich source for clinical interpretation of the individual case, but the difficulty of finding an objective and reliable method of scoring these productions has limited their utility for nonclinical analysis.

Paolino, in dealing with aggression, has focused on an area in which a great deal of research on sex differences has already taken place. For example, Oetzel (1966) noted more than 60 such studies. Virtually all of them agree that boys are more aggressive than girls and men more aggressive than women in all cases of aggression except the verbal variety, where girls occasionally outscore boys. Moreover, women and girls consistently give evidence of greater anxiety and guilt about aggression than men and boys do. Some of the best studies in this area have been done by Buss (1961), who views this trait quite differently from the currently popular ethological approaches of Lorenz (1963) or Ardrey (1966).

It should perhaps be noted that, like Erikson, Paolino encounters some difficulty with his statistical analyses. Specifically, the values of the standard deviations for aggression scores in his Table 1 suggest that, in almost all cases, males are significantly more *variable* in this regard than females. That is, although most males achieve higher aggression scores than most females, *some* males are probably less aggressive than *any* females. This finding which supports Ellis' theory of greater male variability is a bit difficult to interpret, but it does not appear inconsistent with Freud's view of the function of repression.

Freud suggested that both the *strength* and the *locus* of repression could differ from one individual to another: thoughts or feelings that might be intensely repressed by one individual could be much less, or not at all, repressed by another. Furthermore, he argued that *males* tend to repress Oedipal material, and elements associated with Oedipal material, far more than females. In *some* males, then, one may expect that *any* kind of aggressive material is associated with Oedipal conflicts to such an extent that it is censored either from a dream itself or from

Journal of Projective Techniques, 1964, **28**, 219-226. Based on a portion of a doctoral dissertation submitted to the Department of Psychology, Western Reserve University.

later recollection of the dream. In other males, in whom aggression is not so closely linked to Oedipal conflicts, motives for the expression of aggressive material would lead to its appearance. Because of the more direct relationship of aggression to sexuality in the male, (as compared to the female), either of these extreme positions will probably occur more often than the compromise or middle position. The greater variability of Paolino's male sample, as compared to his female sample, gives evidence for this situation.

Although Paolino has never published any further data on this study, he has also attempted to investigate specific sexual imagery in the dreams of his subjects (personal communication). He found that nearly half the men in his sample "reported frank sexual actions involving themselves and females," whereas "only one of the 1,693 women's dreams contained a frank sexual action, and this . . . was at the level of sexual desire."

"I felt that women (college age, unmarried) would dream of sex in another form, so to speak, as aggressive attacks by men in which the subject was the victim. Therefore the findings on aggression for the women that bear on this issue might not necessarily suggest that women are passive victims. Rather, these results might be based on the culturally based necessity for women to disguise sexuality as this kind of aggression. After all, in the sexual act, a woman risks pregnancy, which is potent reason for the disguise." If indeed it is fear of pregnancy that leads the woman to feel "aggressed against" in the sexual act, it would be curious to investigage whether the introduction of the Pill has resulted in a change in the content of women's dreams.

Summary: The dream series of 42 male college students and 42 female college students were analyzed for occurrence of aggressive actions in terms of (a) frequency, (b) direction, whether initiated from the dreamer or directed to the dreamer, (c) characters in the dream who were aggressors or victims, and (d) intensity. These variables were further analyzed in terms of their occurrence in the men's dreams and then in the women's dreams with these results:

1. The analysis of dreams for sex differences in aggression shows that (a) men are more aggressive than, and initiate more aggression than, the women, (b) men and women do not differ in amount of aggressive actions they receive, (c) men exceed the women in average intensity of aggression, and exceed the women in aggression initiated or received by them in dreams.

2. Men initiate as much aggression as they receive. Aggressive actions received by the men are more intense than those they initiated.

3. The men involve as their most frequent aggressors or victims, (a) males, (b) people their own age or of unknown age, and (c) people who are strangers.

4. Women receive more aggression than they initiate. They receive more intense aggressive actions than they initiate.

5. The women employ as both aggressors and victims, (a) people of both sexes, (b) people who are about the same age as the dreamer or whose age is not specified in the dream report, and (c) people who are either familiar to the dreamer or strangers.

6. (a) The men employ males to a greater degree than the women, while the women employ females to a greater degree than the men in all aggressive actions. (b) The women receive more aggression from people older than themselves than the men, while the men receive more aggression from people whose age is unspecified than the women. No sex differences are found in aggression initiated by the men and women involving older people, those who are their own age, or people whose age is unspecified. (c) The men receive more aggression from strangers than the women, while the women receive more aggression from familiar people than the men. (d) The men and women do not differ in aggression directed towards familiar people.

For frequency of aggressive actions it is suggested that like the TAT, dreams tend to "mirror" the real life situation of the individual insofar as aggression is concerned, but in addition, especially with men, dreams serve as a means of aggression that rarely, if ever, finds outlet in the waking state of the dreamer. The involvement of the familiar people and strangers in aggression was explained on the basis of residual ego functioning which operates so that familiar people are placed in a context of minor aggression and strangers are placed in a context of serious aggression.

That there are relatively few normative studies in the area of dreams (Blanchard, 1926; Husband, 1936; Kimmins, 1920; Kinsey et al., 1948, 1953) may be due to the influence of the usual method of dream interpretation (Freud, 1900, 1925) which is concerned with the analysis of the latent rather than manifest content of dreams. Hall (1947) notes that analysis of the manifest content of a series of dreams has proven to be useful in personality assessment, and his scheme of analysis for dream series has been employed in various studies (Polster, 1950; Pope, 1952; Meer, 1955). This analysis, which represents a method of appraising personality, is based on the proposition that dreams mirror the conceptions, conflicts (Hall, 1953), and thus the personality dynamics of the dreamer in the same way as projective techniques. Other investigators have employed the manifest content of dreams in connection with other variables (Gordon, 1954; Sarason, 1944). In view of the continuing interest in dreams in research, a study was undertaken to investigate the manifest content of dreams of college students of both sexes. The present investigation is an empirical study of manifest dream narratives of college men and women, with particular focus[1] on the aggressive actions in the dream reports, analyzed in terms of frequency and intensity of these actions and in

[1]In the larger study of aggression, friendliness, misfortunes and miscellaneous actions in dreams it was found that characters in dreams younger than the dreamer, prominent people, or animals were not present in sufficient quantity to permit meaningful statistical calculations. In addition, there were only few actions such as aggression or friendliness where the dreamer did not participate or was an observer.

terms of the figures in the dream who instigate or are the victims of the aggressive actions.

Method of Procedure

The subjects in this study were 42 female and 42 male undergraduate college students who had completed a course in Introductory Psychology and were currently enrolled in a personality and adjustment class. The subjects were matched for age with an approximate mean age of 21 years, school grade, religion, marital status, and socio-economic level. They were also roughly matched as to whether both parents were present, mother or father absent, or whether they had younger or older siblings or were only children.

The subjects were asked to record their dreams as soon as possible after awakening on printed forms provided for them by instructors in psychology at Western Reserve University.

The mean number of dreams in the series of dreams reported by each subject was 15.5 with a range of 7 to 21, with no significant difference between the male and female groups in the mean number of dreams in the series. The women's dreams contained a mean of 40.3 characters in each dream series, significantly more than the mean of 27.2 characters in each of the men's dream series.

Each of the dreams was scored blindly by the writer in accordance with Hall's (1949) scoring manual. The people in the dream were categorized according to sex, age, and their relationship to the dreamer. Each aggressive act occurring in the dream was scored as to whether the subject was the aggressor or whether he was the victim of the aggressive act. The characteristics, age, sex, and relationship of the people in the dream who initiated or were the object of each aggressive act were also tabulated. Each act was scored for increasing intensity, scaled one through eight, according to the following scheme:

1. Feeling hostile but no outward expression.
2. Expressing hostility verbally, by looks, or by gestures.
3. Preventing from doing something, refusing to do something, being disobedient.
4. Serious accusation or threat.
5. Stealing or destroying, or attempting to do these things, arresting.
6. Chasing, kidnapping, holding prisoner, about to attack.
7. Physical attack or punishment, shooting, attempting to kill.
8. Intentional killing.

The inter-rater reliability of this scheme has been discussed elsewhere (Meer, 1955) with obtained correlations between scorers of

.95 for frequency and .93 for intensity of aggressive acts. A correlation of .98 was obtained between the scoring of the writer and an independent scorer in both the frequency and intensity of aggressive actions.

The aggressive acts which the subject himself initiates, e.g., "I struck the man," are called aggression from the dreamer. Actions in which the subject is the victim, e.g., "The man struck me," are called aggressions to the dreamer. Since each aggressive action involves a person in the dream either as victim or aggressor, the total number of such actions is divided by the total number of people appearing in series of dreams for each subject, yielding a ratio of aggressive actions per character.

The average intensity of aggression is obtained by dividing the total intensity of aggressive actions by the frequency of all aggressive actions in each series of dreams. These measures made it possible to compare the amount of aggression initiated by the subject in his dreams, aggression from dreamer, with the amount of aggression he received, aggression to dreamer. Similarly, comparisons could be made between the average intensity of aggression he instigated in his dream series and the average intensity of aggression which he received. Because of the skewed nature of these measures non-parametric tests of significance were used in this study. The Wilcoxon Rank difference test was employed for these comparisons within each group of subjects and the Mann-Whitney U-test was used for determination of sex differences for the aggressive ratios and average intensities of aggression.

The amount of aggression the subject manifested in his series of dreams was then further analyzed, first to determine which proportion of the total number of aggressive actions involved males, females, or people whose sex was not specified. Similarly, the proportions of aggression involving people whose ages were older, the same as, or unspecified, and the proportions of aggression involving people who were either familiar to the subject or strangers to him were obtained. The same non-parametric tests were employed in analyzing these data.

Results

The upper portion of Table 1 presents the ratios of aggressive actions divided by the number of characters in the series of dreams for the men and the women, while the lower portion gives the average intensity of the aggression.

Table 1. Comparison of Vectors of Aggression for Average Intensity and Aggressive Acts per Character with Sex Differences.

		Total			To-Dreamer			From-Dreamer		
	n	Mean	SD	n	Mean	SD	n	Mean	SD	p
Men's dreams	42	.24	.18	37	.11	.10	37	.12	.10	NS
Women's dreams	41	.13	.08	38	.08	.06	34	.05	.04	.01
p		.01			NS			.01		

		Average Intensity of Aggression								
		Total			To-Dreamer			From-Dreamer		
	n	Mean	SD	n	Mean	SD	n	Mean	SD	p
Men's dreams	42	4.5	1.4	37	4.7	1.3	37	4.1	2.1	.01
Women's dreams	41	3.4	1.2	38	4.1	1.5	34	2.5	1.7	.01
p		.01			.05			.05		

The most striking finding is that while 42 men and only one less woman, 41, all show some aggression in their dreams, men are more aggressive than women, with a ratio of .24 aggressive actions per character versus a ratio of .13 for the women. Stating these findings another way, the men involve about one out of each four people in aggressive actions, while the women involve about one out of eight people in aggression. The upper portion of Table 1 shows that the men and women do not differ in amount of aggression they receive, ratios of .11 and .08 respectively of aggression to the dreamer. On the other hand, the men initiate more aggression than the women, ratios of .12 and .05 respectively of aggression from the dreamer.

In the lower portion of Table 1 it can be seen that the men show a greater intensity of aggression than the women, with an average intensity of 4.5 significantly greater than the average intensity of 3.4 for the women. The intensity of aggression for the men involves serious accusations, threats or more aggressive actions, while the intensity of aggression for the women involves disobedience or refusals to comply. The men also receive more severe aggressive actions (to dreamer) than the women, with an average intensity of 4.7 and 4.1 respectively. The difference is more outstanding when the men are compared with the women for average intensity of aggression which they instigate, 4.1 and 2.5 respectively.

When the aggression shown by the men is compared for differences in amount instigated or received, Table 1 shows that there is no significant difference, a ratio of .11 to the dreamer and .12 from the dreamer. The women, however, receive more aggression than they give, with ratios of .08 (to the dreamer) and .05 (from the dreamer) respectively. Table 1 also shows that the men receive more serious aggression than they give, with an average intensity of 4.7 (to the dreamer) and 4.1 (from the dreamer) respectively. The same holds for the women where they receive more serious aggression, an average of 4.1, than they give, an average of 2.5.

Table 2 shows that 64.6 per cent of all the aggression the men receive comes from males, which is significantly more than the 44.4 per cent of aggression which the women receive from males. On the other hand, the women receive more aggression from females, 29.5 per cent, than do the men with 9.2 per cent.

Table 2. Sex Differences in Mean Percentages of Aggressive Actions for the Character Categories Divided by Sex, Age, and Relationship.

Character Categories	Character Sub-categories	Aggression To-Dreamer				Aggression From-Dreamer			
		Men's Dreams	Women's Dreams	z	p	Men's Dreams	Women's Dreams	z	p
Sex	Male	64.6	44.4	2.23	.05	70.2	40.7	2.41	.05
	Female	9.2	29.5	3.06	.01	11.2	32.7	2.85	.01
	Sex not specified	25.9	26.4	.01	NS	18.2	27.0	.77	NS
Age	Older	6.7	24.7	3.46	.01	9.5	19.2	1.13	NS
	Peer	22.7	26.2	.60	NS	34.7	40.5	.69	NS
	Age not specified	71.5	49.9	2.81	.01	54.8	40.2	1.38	NS
Relation-ship	Familiar	21.7	40.3	2.74	.01	27.3	47.8	1.86	NS
	Strangers	66.2	46.5	2.98	.01	53.7	42.7	.98	NS
	Relation not specified	12.1	13.1	.72	NS	18.9	9.4	1.56	NS

In aggression initiated by the men, 70.2 per cent involves male victims which is significantly less than the 40.7 per cent of aggression directed by the women towards male victims. On the other hand, the women direct 32.7 per cent of their aggression towards female victims, significantly more than the 11.2 per cent directed by the men towards female victims. A substantial percentage of all aggression shown by both men and women involved people whose sex is not specified in the dream reports, with no significant differences in this sub-category of characters.

Insofar as age of people involved in aggression is concerned, only two significant differences are seen in Table 2, where the women receive more aggression from older people than the men, 24.7 per cent and 6.7 per cent respectively, and where the men receive more aggression from people whose age is unknown than do the women, 71.5 per cent and 49.9 per cent respectively.

The women receive more aggression from familiar people than the men, 40.3 per cent and 21.7 per cent respectively, and the men receiving more aggression than the women from strangers, 66.2 per cent and 46.5 per cent respectively.

It can be seen from Table 3 that the men involve males in their aggressive actions, receiving 64.6 per cent from males and directing 70.2 per cent towards males, which is significantly more than the percentages of aggression involving females, 9.2 per cent and 11.2 per cent respectively. It may be of interest to add that analysis of data on which Table 3 is based showed that 40 out of the 42 men involved male characters in aggression while significantly far less men, 16, involved female characters in aggression.

Table 3. Comparison of Mean Percentages of Aggressive Actions for the Dream Characters Divided by Sex, Age, and Relationship.

Character Categories	n	Aggression Vector	Men's Dreams A	B	C	Pab*	Pac*	Pbc*
			Male	Female	Sex Not Specified			
Sex	37	To-Dreamer	64.6	9.2	25.9	.01	.05	NS
	37	From-Dreamer	70.2	11.2	18.2	.01	.01	NS
			Older	Peer	Age Not Specified	Pab*	Pac*	Pbc*
Age	37	To-Dreamer	6.7	22.7	71.5	NS	.01	.01
	37	From-Dreamer	9.5	34.7	54.8	.05	.01	NS
			Familiar	Stranger	Relation Not Specified	Pab*	Pac*	Pbc*
Relationship	37	To-Dreamer	21.7	66.2	12.1	.01	NS	.01
	37	From-Dreamer	27.3	53.7	18.9	.05	NS	.01

Character Categories	n	Aggression Vector	Women's Dreams A	B	C	Pab*	Pac*	Pbc*
			Male	Female	Sex Not Specified			
Sex	38	To-Dreamer	44.4	29.5	26.4	NS	NS	NS
	34	From-Dreamer	40.7	32.7	27.0	NS	NS	NS
			Older	Peer	Age Not Specified	Pab*	Pac*	Pbc*
Age	38	To-Dreamer	24.7	26.2	49.9	NS	.01	NS
	34	From-Dreamer	19.2	40.5	40.2	.05	.01	NS
			Familiar	Stranger	Relation Not Specified	Pab*	Pac*	Pbc*
Relationship	38	To-Dreamer	40.3	46.5	13.1	NS	.01	.01
	34	From-Dreamer	47.8	42.7	9.4	NS	.01	.01

*Significance values for comparison, of columns A with B, A with C, and B with C with each comparison indicated by subscript.

Table 3 shows that the men receive 71.5 per cent of aggressive actions from people whose age is unknown, significantly more than the percentages from people who are his own age or older. Similarly, the men direct 54.8 per cent of aggressive actions towards people whose age is unknown, which is significantly more than the percentage of aggression directed towards older people, 9.5, although not significantly more than the percentage 34.7, directed towards people who are his own age. From the same table it can be seen that the men receive 66.2 per cent of all aggressive acts from strangers, significantly more than the percentages of aggression coming from either familiar people or people whose relationship is not specified. Similarly, the men direct 53.7 per cent significantly more aggression towards strangers than familiar people or those whose relationship is not specified.

Reading horizontally in Table 3 it can be seen that the women receive 44.4 per cent of all aggressive actions from males, 29.5 per cent from females, and 26.4 per cent from people whose sex is not specified. No significant differences are found in proportion of aggression directed towards males, females, or people whose sex is unknown.

The women receive 49.9 per cent of aggression from people whose age is not specified significantly more than the percentage received from people older than the subject. The women direct 40.2 per cent of their aggression to people whose age is not specified and to people their own age, 40.5 per cent, both significantly more than the percentage directed towards older people. No significant difference is found in percentages of aggression coming from familiar people or strangers.

Discussion

The most striking finding in this study of aggression is the greater frequency and higher average intensity of aggression in the dreams of men than in the dreams of women. This result would be in accord with what might be expected on the basis of psychoanalytic theory of psychosexual development (Freud, 1925) wherein differences in oedipal development increase masculinity in the male, and increase femininity in the female. Since dreams purport to tap the unconscious, then such differences in masculinity, passivity, and aggression are most likely to be expressed in the dream. However, the greater frequency and intensity of aggression in the men's dreams might also be expected if a cultural conception of personality were accepted. Men who are more aggressive due to their cultural role and cultural expectations, express more hostility in dreams, while women who are more passive due to identifications with the prevailing role of womanhood (Mead, 1949) will express less hostility in dreams.

The men show no difference in amounts of aggression they initiate or they receive. Psychoanalytic theory might predict that the amount of aggression initiated by the men should outweigh the aggression they receive because of the greater masculinity based on differences in oedipal development. A more parsimonious explanation may be that the male, who is more aggressive in our society, will express this aggression towards other men, who, in real life, may be as aggressive in return. The women, on the other hand, receive more aggression than they initiate which might be expected from the social role of women who are less assertive and more passive than men. The dream, therefore, seems to reflect the way in which aggression is initiated or received by both the men and the women in daily life.

Insofar as sex differences are concerned, we find that men exceed the women in amounts of aggression they initiate. So, again, the men, who are more aggressive in real life, initiate more aggression in dreams than the women who, themselves, are less aggressive in real life, thereby mirroring the real life differences in aggression. Related to this finding are the results of TAT studies (Gordon, 1954) where fantasied aggression is found to be positively correlated with the overt expression of this need.

The average intensity of aggression in women's dreams is at a socially accepted verbal level, while that for the men's dreams is at the socially discouraged level of stealing, destruction of property, and even injury or death. While the women's dreams tend to reflect the same intensity of hostility shown by women in real life, the greater intensity of hostility in the men may be explained by the fact that under certain conditions, such as in self-defense or while functioning as a soldier or policeman, men can justifiably injure or even kill. However, the occasions for expression of such intense hostility are so infrequent, even if permitted under these specific conditions, that the dream can be said to provide the male dreamer an opportunity for release of serious extrapunitive hostility that he rarely, if ever, manifests in daily life.

Aggression is not a disembodied force in dream analysis but is scored in the dyadic relationship between the dreamer and the people in the dream, and the vehicles for expression of aggression are these characters in the dream. The men tend to use males as agents or victims of aggression while the women tend to use people of both sexes in aggression. An explanation of this result may be found in the greater intensity of aggression found in men's dreams where males, the culturally accepted agents of serious aggression, are so employed in the dream. On the other hand, women who show less intense aggression in dreams can use both males and females with impunity, since in our culture people of both sexes are likely as not to initiate or become the victim of such minor aggressive acts as "dirty looks" or verbal criticism. For the dreams of men and women our results tend to reflect what is acceptable in our culture, yet, since murder, physical injury and such are often expressed in the dreams of the men in our sample, it must be assumed that dreams can also serve as a means of expressing socially suppressed impulses.

Psychoanalytical theories might explain the sex differences in the people involved in aggression, especially in the men's dreams, where almost no aggression involved females. These results are in accord with what might be expected after the resolution of the oedipus conflict in men, who do not pass through a hostile phase to the mother, and whose castration fears may result in hostility towards, or fear of, father figures. Women, who in the resolution of their focal conflict pass through a phase of hostility towards both father and mother, might just as likely select female characters, as well as males, as aggressors or victims.

Insofar as age of the people involved in aggression is concerned, the predominant aggressors or victims in both men's and women's dreams are persons who are the same age as the dreamer or those whose age cannot be specified by the dreamer. The inability to specify the age of the aggressors or victims may be based in the processes of Dream-Work (Freud, 1900), which may becloud such details as age, and/or relationship of the aggressors or victims, especially if the aggressive intensity is particularly frightening to the dreamer. The women show more aggression coming from older people than do the men, which may be accounted for by the fact that their average intensity of aggression is at a low level, permitting the dreamer to distinguish the age of the aggressor. In the men, their more intense aggression may obscure such details of the aggressor as age and relationship.

An "ego-functioning" explanation may clarify the results regarding the dreamer's relationship to the people involved in aggression. The men use strangers in their highly intense aggression while the women use both familiar and strange people in their comparatively minor level of aggression. In real life one does not ordinarily involve family or friends in serious aggression, so in the dream the same social inhibitions may force the choice of strangers in seriously aggressive acts. Perhaps some form of ego-functioning still is effective in the dreaming state, forcing serious aggression to be manifest with strangers and permitting minor aggression to involve the family or friends of the dreamer. Involving strangers in aggression is more socially acceptable than involving people close to the dreamer, as is borne out in studies of prejudice where hostility is most commonly manifest towards the out-group rather than towards the in-group members. The approximate formula for the residual ego-functioning in dreams suggested here is that the more serious the aggression where the dreamer is either agent or victim, the greater is the amount of "disguise" in age and relationship of the dream characters.

Walter A. Kaess
Sam L. Witryol

Memory for Names and Faces: A Characteristic of Social Intelligence?

The topic of sex differences in social sensitivity and dependence has been almost as well researched as that of sex differences in aggression, which is its logical counterpart. Oetzel (1966) listed about 50 studies in this area. In almost all of them, girls proved to be more socially sensitive or dependent.

Kaess and Witryol's study approaches this topic from a slightly different angle—that of assessing social intelligence, as distinct from ordinary intelligence. Presumably, people who show a talent for associating names with faces may be intrinsically more motivated to learn this kind of material.

This form of analysis of male-female differences has a long history. As early as the 1920s, Moore (1922), Landis (1927), and Landis and Burtt (1924) attempted to discern sex differences by analyzing the topics and mannerisms of everyday conversations overheard in the streets. Carlson, Cook, and Stromberg (1936) and Watson, Breed, and Posman (1948) continued these investigations, all with consistent results: Men talk about money, business, and sports; women talk about other women and clothes. All these studies, as well as Kaess and Witryol's, document Bennett and Cohen's fourth principle: Men value achievement, and women value social love and friendship.

This experiment was designed to analyze factors which are related to performance on the Memory for Names and Faces subtest of the George Washington University Social Intelligence Test (Moss, Hunt, Omwake, & Woodward, 1949). One might, but probably should not, say that the memory-for-names-and-faces type of test has high face validity. The basic experimental task requires the subject to associate a name with a face. The testee is asked to memorize the names of a number of portrait photographs. Later, the testee is given a larger group of photographs and requested to identify the pictures previously studied. Most testees and not a few employment managers assume that this type of test measures a useful social skill. Many indi-

Journal of Applied Psychology, 1955, **39**, 457-462. © 1955 by the American Psychological Association and reproduced by permission.

viduals who successfully deal with large numbers of people are reputed to have phenomenal memories for names and faces. Presumably the ability to say, "Hello, Mr. Piccalilli, I believe we met eight years ago in the elevator at Radio City," serves as an ego-inflating stimulus which tends to make Mr. Piccalilli more likely to buy an insurance policy or cast a vote for a particular candidate. Presumably, also, to address Mr. Piccalilli as Mr. Mustard will be taken as a direct assault upon his person, and the sale or the vote will be irretrievably lost.

Tests requiring the association of a name with a face enjoy considerable popularity. Besides being included in the George Washington scale, this type of test is included in the Factored Aptitude Series (King, 1947) which is reportedly used by many industrial organizations. The manual of the latter states, ". . . the ability measured is broader than test content. Good memory for names and faces also means ability to recall other types of information." Performance on the memory-for-faces test is reported by the manual to be related to performance on such jobs as: agent, buyer, manager, receptionist, salesman, telephone operator, and waiter.

The memory-for-faces type of test has a long history in psychology beginning as early as 1926 (Moss, 1926) when it was incorporated in the first form of the George Washington University Social Intelligence Test. Successive revisions of this scale continued to include this names-and-faces subtest, as does the present form (Moss et al. 1949). One of the authors of the scale, F. A. Moss, defined social intelligence as ". . . the ability to get along with people." He wrote (1926, p. 26): "One of the most important factors in social intelligence is the ability to recognize faces and remember names. The person who gets along best with others does not have to be introduced to a man three or four times before he remembers that he has met him before." Probably the best critical summaries of early research on the total scale and the particular subtest under consideration here are contained in the reviews by Thorndike and Stein (1937) and by Jackson (1940). The major inferences drawn from this early research were that the test is of dubious validity and that a meaningful criterion of social intelligence had not been definitively isolated.

Important questions remain to be answered concerning this type of memory test. It is not clear exactly what the test is measuring. Does it measure some aspect of social intelligence, general memory, general intelligence, or spatial ability? The sometimes reported differences between various occupational groups are not particularly convincing, since a number of factors could account for the differences.

We have not attempted a direct assault upon the difficult problem of the validity of this type of test. Rather, we have studied aspects of test performance which should hold if the test is to have general utility. The first question studied relative to validity concerned the generality of the ability measured. Does the ability to form strong printed name-photograph associations correlate highly with the ability to form person-spoken name associations which are most common in everyday life? Our second question considered whether the instructions to the testee may not in themselves destroy the very thing the test wishes to measure. When we say, "Study these pictures carefully because . . . ," do we not establish a preparatory set in even the most self-centered individual so strong that his performance represents rote memory rather than some aspect of social memory? The third question regarding the existence and extent of sex differences was suggested from the previous literature and from early exploratory efforts in the present investigation.

Experimental Procedure

The subjects in this investigation were 111 males and 99 females enrolled in nine laboratory sections of the Introductory Psychology course at the University of Connecticut. The average lab section size was 23. Data collected from measures on students in this course on the Allport-Vernon Study of Values in recent years have been in very close agreement with the composite norms of American college students published in the manual. Similar representative results have been obtained from scores on group tests of general intelligence. As defined by these measures and published norms, the population at this university appears to be quite representative of American college students.

The Memory for Names and Faces subtest of the George Washington University Social Intelligence Test (GWU) and a names-and-faces miniature life situation were presented to all the lab sections in counterbalanced order. When the GWU subtest was presented first, the instructions served as a set for this task and the miniature situation to follow (Condition I). In those sections where the miniature situation was presented first, instructional set was counterbalanced with no instructions or lack of set (Conditions II and III). Set groups were instructed (Condition II):

"This lab will be a demonstration of a test of social intelligence. I shall give each of these ten people an alias, a false name. When I interview them later, in a sort of radio show of the sidewalk interview type, each will use only his alias, not his real name.

98 Intrapersonal and Interpersonal Behavior

"Listen carefully, for later on you will be asked to remember the alias used by each subject."

Table 1 demonstrates the manner in which this was done. Reference hereafter to experimental conditions will be made in terms of the labels employed in the table: (a) *GWU* for the Memory for Names and Faces subtest, (b) *Interview* for the miniature situation, (c) *Interview Set* for the miniature situation with instructions, and (d) *Interview Non-set* for the miniature situation without instructions.

Table 1. Order of Presentation for Names and Faces (GWU) and Miniature Life Situation (Interview).

Order of Presentation	Condition	Lab Sections
GWU–Interview	I	A, B, C (*N*s = 19, 22, 31)
Interview Set–GWU	II	D, E, F (*N*s = 21, 25, 25)
Interview Non-set–GWU	III	G, H, I (*N*s = 18, 22, 27)

As indicated earlier, on the GWU subtest the testee is asked to memorize the names under 12 picture portraits of young men. Later the 12 pictures are presented again with 13 additional portraits. From this matrix the testee is required to associate the correct one of four pictures presented in multiple-choice form with each of the 12 names. Each correct multiple-choice association is scored one, with a total maximum score of 12.

Five males and five females in each laboratory section were participants in the miniature social situations. Each was assigned an alias by the lab instructor who conducted a very brief "sidewalk interview" for about one minute. In every case it was made certain that the participant-subjects spoke his alias clearly at least once. Later the students in the lab section were asked to match the correct name from the 10 aliases listed on the blackboard with the person who had adopted that name for the experiment. The participant-subjects were presented to the class in a prescribed random order to be identified from one of the names on the blackboard. Although the 10 participant-subjects were different for each of the nine lab sections, the 10 names used as aliases remained standard for all the groups. A score of one was credited for each correct matching. The total maximum score was 10.

It should be noted again that two conditions (I and II) served as a set for the miniature social situation in six of the laboratory sections (see Table 1). The instructions for the GWU subtest provided a set when the Interview task was administered second (Condition I). When the Interview was administered first, set and non-set groups were counterbalanced. Set groups were given instructions as indicated above (Condition II), while non-set groups did not receive any kind of preparatory instructions (Condition III).

The three conditions permitted some evaluation of the effect of instructions upon test and interview performance. If instructions produce marked changes in test scores, the question arises as to which preparatory set-inducing situation provides the most useful measure. The miniature situation provided two groups who experienced a more "lifelike" situation than the paper-and-pencil test afforded. The students who observed the demonstration resembled those who heard but were not the direct recipients of social introductions. The students who were introduced to the class were perhaps one step closer to the more common situation of being an active participant in a social situation. If performance on the GWU subtest measures an ability of considerable generality, it seems reasonable to expect fairly high correlations between the GWU and the miniature situations.

Finally, the digit-span subtest from the Wechsler-Bellevue Intelligence Scale was administered to 76 subjects in order to examine the relationship between memory, as defined by recalling digits, and social recall, as defined by the GWU and Interview tasks employed in this investigation.

Results

A detailed analysis in terms of experimental conditions and sex is shown in Table 2. The observer-participant classification is omitted from the present analysis. The means for observers and participants were 6.09 and 6.15, respectively. Although parallel analyses for observer and participant classifications were made, the distinction contributed no additional information, while the effects of the other variables remained in agreement with the other analyses. Except to

Table 2. Summary of Differences between Sexes within Conditions of Set for Interview and GWU.

			Interview			GWU		
Condition	Sex	N	M	SD	t	M	SD	t
I. GWU–Interview	Males	32	5.81	2.39	2.30*	9.28	2.08	0.55
	Females	40	7.05	2.17		9.55	2.08	
	Both sexes	72	6.50	2.27		9.43	2.08	
II. Interview Set– GWU	Males	41	5.32	2.33	2.98**	9.73	1.90	2.04*
	Females	30	7.03	2.47		10.60	1.61	
	Both sexes	71	6.04	2.39		10.10	1.78	
III. Interview Non- set–GWU	Males	38	5.50	2.51	2.77**	8.18	2.19	3.59***
	Females	29	7.17	2.33		10.31	2.65	
	Both sexes	67	6.22	2.44		9.10	2.40	

*.05 level of confidence.
**.01 level of confidence.
***.001 level of confidence.

illustrate special points, the following results are based on all subjects, $N=210$:

1. *Analysis of miniature social situation.* Sex differences on the Interview tasks demonstrated female superiority and were consistent for all three conditions. However, there were no differences in task performance as a function of the three experimental conditions of set. A double analysis of variance[1] yielded an F of 23.02 (F .001 = 11.38) between sexes, while the mean square between conditions of set was smaller than the error term or the almost nonexistent interaction.

2. *Analysis of memory for names and faces.* Analysis of variance demonstrated female superiority on the GWU subtest. The F between sexes was 12.37 (F .001 = 11.38). The mean squares for the three conditions of set, and for the sex and set interaction, were near the .05 level of confidence. These results are not as clear-cut as the comparable analyses for the Interview tasks above. Sex differences on the GWU subtest appear real from the fact of statistical significance in two of the three conditions; the possible interaction is regarded as the result of uncontrolled factors among the males in Condition III. The evidence for influence upon scores by the three experimental conditions of set is slight.

3. *Analysis of sex differences.* The magnitude of the sex differences on both tasks was surprising. For all conditions the female mean score was .67 sigma units above the male mean for the interview, and .49 sigma units above the male mean for the GWU subtest. Only 24 per cent of the female Interview scores were below the male mean, and 30 per cent of the female GWU scores were below the male mean on the latter task. Biserial r's between sex and Interview and between sex and GWU were .418 and .307, respectively (N = 210); these were calculated as an illustrative device for emphasizing the magnitude of the sex differences.

4. *Relationships between tasks.* The Pearson product-moment correlation obtained between the Interview and GWU tasks was .315 (p = .001) for the 210 subjects in the total population. This coefficient is somewhat inflated as a result of combining heterogeneous groups. Thus, when the population was divided into homogeneous sex groupings, the correlation coefficient dropped to .273 for the 111 males and .250 for the 99 females, both coefficients significant at the .01 level. The correlations within conditions were: .237 when the GWU served as a set (Condition I), .276 with Interview set instructions (Condition II), and .451 with no set (Condition III). The tendency indicated in this sequence for the relationships to increase as

---

[1]Bartlett's test for homogeneity of variance and Snedecor's (1946) suggestions for analyzing data having disproportionate subgroups were used for all the analyses of variance.

the strength of preparatory set decreases is suggestive but not statistically significant.

5. *Digit recall relationships and sex differences.* The Wechsler digit-span subtest mean for 39 males was 11.62; and for 37 females it was 12.14, with *SD*'s of 1.93 and 1.90, respectively (t = 1.18). Four product-moment correlations calculated for each sex between the digit-recall test and each of the two social memory tasks were approximately zero: for the males, $-$ .10 and $-$ .09 between digit recall and Interview and GWU subtest, respectively; for the females, $-$ .13 and $-$ .05. Thus, ability to remember names and faces does not appear to be related to the ability to recall another type of information as defined by the digit-span test, nor are the sex differences on the social recall tasks reflected in similar differences on the digit-recall task.

Discussion and Conclusions

The correlations between the miniature social situation and the GWU names-and-faces tasks may be interpreted as an important indication of the generality of the latter scale. The magnitude of the relationships, though small, are of high statistical significance. Thus, there appears to be some generality in the ability measured by the GWU names-and-faces subtest. Possibly the magnitudes of these correlations would be raised if the reliability of the interviews were increased by increasing the number of the participant-subjects (lengthening the test), or by careful rehearsal on the part of the experimenter in each lab section. However, this is not vital to the problem investigated, because the aim of the present study was to evaluate the generality of the GWU subtest rather than to develop a parallel form for it. It is doubtful that the relatively low relationships found between the GWU and the rather uniform interviews would be higher with "reality" criteria where innumerable factors are uncontrolled. It appears, then, that a memory-for-faces type of test possibly measures a useful social skill, but lacks in its present form sufficient generality to have widespread practical application.

The magnitudes of the sex differences on both experimental tasks suggests a statistical contamination not always clarified in research on social intelligence and social perception. If females are superior to males on several tasks, any correlations computed on these measures will be spuriously inflated when groups of mixed sex are studied. Exemplary is the attenuation of the .315 coefficient of correlation between the two names-and-faces tests for the mixed population of 210. When the same relationships were calculated for each of the sexes, the coefficients dropped to .273 and .250 for males and females, respectively. Without this logical correction it is possible that scores on the Interview and GWU tasks might be related to a test of verbal ability because females tend to be superior on this latter task also. In some situations factor analyses of mixed sex populations could result in factor loadings highly contaminated by sex differences. Conceivably, then, one could indicate a clear-cut factor, employ tests with high loadings to name the factor, and yet completely overlook the possibility of measuring the factor by observing whether the testee wears lipstick! The combination of heterogeneous groups can yield spurious relationships leading to serious misconceptions in interpretation.

It is difficult to account for the findings in the present investigation regarding the female superiority on both tasks. Early research on the GWU subtest indicated no sex differences (Moss & Hunt, 1927; Hunt, 1928; Woodrow, 1939) although sex differences for the total score and for other subtests of the scale were found. Some evidence reporting social intelligence to have a fairly high loading on the verbal factor (Thorndike, 1936) may be suggestive. On the other hand, Woodrow, who controlled for sex differences, found the GWU names-and-faces test to have highest loadings on a spatial factor (Woodrow, 1939). Furthermore, factors such as intelligence and digit-span memory are unlikely to account for the pronounced sex differences obtained here. Finally, unpublished research on the population employed in this study did not reveal significant sex differences in motivation and interest.

Two alternative and speculative explanations are offered. Most of the previous research has been reported on the old Revised Form, First Edition of the Social Intelligence Test (Moss, Hunt, & Omwake, 1930). In this form, pictures are of males, 30 to 50 years of age, dressed in the archaic style appropriate to the 1920s. By modern standards some of the picture-portraits might be colloquially termed "characters" or "creeps." The most recent form of the test (Moss et al., 1949) is composed of pictures of young men in the 18 to 20 years range. Each looks like an excellent model for a shirt ad in a teenage magazine. Perhaps the change increased the feminine interest. The second and more speculative suggestion is based upon Riesman's concept of the inner- and outer-directed personalities (Riesman, 1950). If the hypothesis is true that there has been a general drift toward outer direction in our time, it is also conceivable that this modification of character has been relatively more accelerated in females. This tentative interpretation stems from the fact that most of the research on the GWU scale was conducted in the late '20s and early '30s. Although both explanations are speculative, the consequences are testable and may be worth further research.

Summary

The Memory for Names and Faces picture subtest of the George Washington University Social Intelligence Test and a miniature social situation testing the association of spoken names with human subjects in a simulated life setting were administered to 210 students in nine Introductory Psychology laboratory sections at the University of Connecticut. Three conditions of set and non-set were also introduced to evaluate the consequences of preparatory instructions upon the social recall task performances. Finally, the digit-recall subtest of the Wechsler-Bellevue scale was administered to 76 subjects in order to explore the similarity between this type of memory function and the two social recall tasks. The evidence from the results in this experiment appear to warrant the following conclusions:

1. The relationships between the social recall tasks are small (about .30) but statistically significant, reflecting some generality; widespread application is seriously limited.
2. Sex differences favoring females on both social recall tasks are highly significant and contradictory to some early research reporting no differences.
3. Set, as defined by preparatory instructions for the two tasks, does not significantly influence performance.
4. The social recall tasks are not related to one type of memory, as measured by the group administration of the Wechsler-Bellevue digit-span subtest.

Two speculative and possibly testable hypotheses were offered to account for some of the findings.

Dirk L. Schaeffer
Joseph Eisenberg

Cognitive Conflict and Compromise between Males and Females

The previous studies in this text have sought and found sex differences in a variety of areas of human behavior; the present study sought but, by and large, failed to find any such differences. As indicated by the studies cited in the introduction to this reading, there was ample reason to expect sex differences in the way male and female subjects responded to conflict and in the ease with which they developed compromises, but the differences were not found.

I can offer a number of explanations, one of the most likely of which is that this experiment might have been biased against the appearance of sex differences. The argument that all subjects were college students and thus presumably equal in intellectual and cognitive capacity appears trivial, since it applies as well to most studies that have found sex differences; yet the fact that this study focused entirely on cognitive processes and only allowed personality factors to emerge within the realm of cognitive maneuvering may have allowed such a bias to operate. Since 10 of the 11 subjects rejected from the experiment for failure to meet the training criterion were

female, it appears not only that sex differences in cognitive capacity (in this particular situation) may exist but also that the use of a training criterion may have obliterated them. On the other hand, studies such as those by Witkin and his associates (Witkin, Dyk, Faterson, Goodenough, & Karp, 1962), dealing with field dependence and related problem-solving tasks, suggest that even in this area sex differences should have been found. Again, however, the use of the training criterion might have wiped them out.

Another explanation is that sex differences in this particular area may not be very significant, and this point is paradoxically supported by those few sex differences that *were* found in the study. Thus the data suggest that properly trained males and females do not differ in the accuracy with which they use judgmental cues, in the amount of conflict they experience in noncompetitive situations, or in the amount of compromise they show; however, they *do* differ in the way they are treated by others: females simply are not so likely as males to be believed when they are trying to communicate a complicated policy.

This report is based in part on a master's thesis submitted to the Department of Psychology, University of Alberta, by the junior author under the supervision of the senior. A brief version of this report was read at the Western Psychological Association Convention, Vancouver, British Columbia, Canada, in June 1969.

This finding is quite consistent with the anecdotal reports of thousands of career women regarding the difficulties they experience in finding professional acceptance in male-dominated occupations. Moreover, the present study provides evidence that is compatible with both Freudian and social learning viewpoints, although its implications (such as the effect that this apparent belief, on the part of both sexes, that women are not competent to think complexly, might have on unconscious attitudes toward child raising) tend more to support the social learning positions.

Abstract. Hammond's (1965) paradigm for the study of cognitive conflict and compromise calls for training two *S*s individually to make judgments about a criterion on the basis of 2 cues: for each *S* one cue is highly relevant, and the other irrelevant, to accurate judgment. Two differently trained *S*s are then brought together for a series of conflict trials, in which they must make individual and joint judgments of the criterion. The present study used 4 groups of 10 pairs each. The groups consisted of males or females trained on a simple (linear) or complex (curvilinear) cue-criterion relationship and paired in the four possible combinations of one linear with one curvilinear *S*. No differences were apparent for any measures of conflict or compromise. However, pairs in which a female was trained on a complex cue appeared less accurate in their judgment than those in which a male was so trained, regardless of the sex of the linearly trained *S*. This finding was interpreted as a further aspect of cultural sex-role stereotyping.

Cognitive conflict arises when an individual is presented with mutually incompatible items of information. Whereas cognitive dissonance (Festinger, 1957) is generally applied to conflicts existing within one individual, cognitive conflict has been studied primarily in interpersonal situations in which two or more persons must use apparently discrepant information to reach a joint decision (Hammond, Todd, Wilkins & Mitchell, 1966; Hammond, 1965, 1969). Also, in studies of cognitive conflict there is no inequality in the reinforcement or reward given to *S*s.

Research with Hammond's (1965) cognitive conflict paradigm has, to date, been restricted to all-male samples. His most extensive study of cognitive conflict (Hammond, 1967) utilized a judgmental situation in which one *S* was trained to make relatively simple (linear) judgments while another was trained to make more complex (curvilinear) judgments. Following training, *S*s were brought together to make individual and *joint* judgments on tasks apparently similar to those on which they had been trained. For this last series of judgments, however, outcome feedback was given in such a manner that a 50-50 split of differences in judgments would result in the most accurate responses; thus accuracy of judgment was, to some extent, confounded with willingness to compromise in reaching joint judgments. In this situation, Hammond found that compromise was low at the outset of the 20 joint trials, but rose fairly sharply over the first 10 trials and then leveled off, that there was little increase in joint accuracy over the 20 trials, and that *S*s trained on the relatively complex task showed compromise (or adaptation to the new task demands) more readily than did subjects trained on the relatively simple task.

Available evidence on sex differences suggests that males and females should behave quite differently in situations involving cognitive processes, conflict, and compromise. Several investigators have found that females' cognitive approaches to problems differ from males' in terms of category width (Wallach & Caron, 1959; Wallach & Kagan, 1959), susceptibility to set formation (Guetzkow, 1951; Luchins & Luchins, 1959), deductive reasoning (Kostich, 1954), and problem solving (Nakamura, 1958). In conflict situations, Vinacke and his colleagues (Vinacke, 1959; Bond & Vinacke, 1961; Uesugi & Vinacke, 1963), as well as various researchers employing the Prisoner's Dilemma (Rappoport & Chammah, 1965; Komorita, 1965; Bixenstine & Wilson, 1963; Bixenstine, Chambers, & Wilson, 1963), have found extensive sex differences characterizing male-male, female-female, and mixed-sex pairs or triads. In addition to differences in compromise observed in these studies, Nakamura (1958) and Allen and Crutchfield (1963) among others have found females to be more conforming than males in a variety of judgmental and problem-solving situations.

The present study undertook to test the generality of Hammond's (1967) findings on different sex groups. In view of the many differences discerned between the sexes in both cognitive functioning and the management of conflict, compromise, and conformity, it seemed possible to formulate several hypotheses concerning the differential effects of sexuality on the two critical measures (conflict and accuracy) derived from this paradigm.

1. In general, the overall pattern of initial decline and then leveling off of conflict and the lack of change of joint accuracy should be found since there is nothing in the reported data on sex differences in similar situations to suggest increased conflict or accuracy in all female or mixed-sex groups.

2. Females' greater susceptibility to set formation (Luchins & Luchins, 1959) should lead them to adhere to their original training policies and avoid compromise longer than males.

3. Females' greater willingness to compromise (Bond & Vinacke, 1961) and conform (Allen & Crutchfield, 1963) should lead them to become more accurate and show less conflict than males on later trials.

These last two hypotheses would, then, call for interactions between sex of subject and blocks of trials in the statistical analyses of these data, with female subjects doing more poorly early in testing, but better later in testing, than males.

4. In mixed-sex groups, the greater willingness of females to compromise would interact with the greater willingness of subjects trained on a relatively complex task to compromise. Thus in groups in which the female has been trained on the complex task she will over-compromise as it were, leading to reduced conflict at the cost of reduced accuracy, while in groups in which the male has been trained on the relatively complex task, both he and his female partner will compromise roughly equally, thus achieving the greatest accuracy.

Method

Design

Hammond's (1965) paradigm for the study of cognitive conflict, based on Brunswik's (1952, 1956) "lens model" of perceptual and judgmental tasks, primarily involves the training of Ss to utilize one of two cues in making a cognitive judgment. The cue-criterion relationship taught to S is probabilistic rather than completely accurate; random error introduced into S's feedback during training prevents him from ever achieving a "perfect" strategy for solving his problem. Two Ss are individually trained in this manner; each is taught to rely on one of the two cues and to disregard the other. They are then brought together on a series of test trials and required to make both individual and joint (compromise) judgments in a situation in which both cues are equally relevant.

For the present study, Hammond's "political judgment" task (Hammond et al., 1966) was used in precisely the same form as Hammond and his colleagues (see also Hammond, Bartoli-Bonaituo, Faucheux, Moscovici, Frohlich, Joyce, & di Majo, 1968) applied it.* In this task Ss are presented with two graphs, which illustrate the amount of "free elections" and level of "state control" in hypothetical nations. They are then asked to judge the "level of democratic institutions" of these nations. In one S's training, the cue of "free elections" is *linearly* related to the criterion, so that increasing values on this cue are associated with increasing values on the criterion; the second cue is irrelevant. For the other S, "state control" is *curvilinearly* related to

*All materials used in this study were supplied by Dr. Kenneth R. Hammond, Institute for Behavioral Sciences (IBS), University of Colorado, and are identical with materials used in prior studies of this paradigm. Grateful acknowledgement is due both to him and to Dr. Monroe J. Miller, also of IBS, for extensive advice and assistance in all phases of this research.

the criterion, so that both low and high values on this cue are associated with low "levels of democratic institutions" and intermediate
values are associated with high "levels of democratic institutions"; for
these Ss the "free elections" cue is irrelevant. Figure 1 graphically
presents these cue-criterion relations, both in training and during the
test phase.

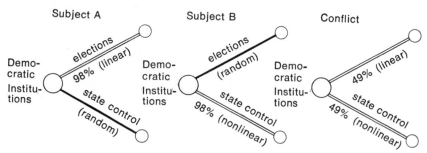

Figure 1. Cue-criterion relationships during training and conflict series.

Training for each S proceeds for 60 trials (or 80 if criterion performance levels are not attained after 60 trials), after which the Ss are
brought together in pairs for 20 conflict trials. In the conflict trials
each cue maintains its linear or nonlinear properties, but both cues
are *equally* relevant to the criterion. Figure 2 illustrates the measures
that can be derived from each trial of the conflict series. Here T represents the response a given S would have made on that trial if he had
followed his training perfectly; the value is found by substituting the

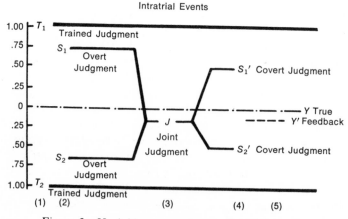

Figure 2. Variables assessed on each training trial.

cue values for that trial into the multiple-regression equation describing his performance on the block of 20 training trials immediately preceding the conflict series. S represents the S's *overt* judgment of the criterion for that trial (given verbally), and J is the joint judgment agreed upon by both members of the pair after discussion. S' is S's *covert* judgment, which is given only to E after the joint decision has been made (S is told that "Since these are real, complex cases, you may still have some reservations about the accuracy of the joint decision"). Y and Y' represent the "correct" compromise judgment for that trial and the feedback given Ss; Y' is evaluated as $Y + e$, where e is random error with a mean of 0 and a standard deviation of 1.

Further scores can be derived from these data (see Table 1). All scores are in terms of absolute values, corrected for the possible range of choices open to Ss on that trial. Several scores are recorrected by means of arc-tangent transformations, which both normalize the distributions and restrict the range of the scores to values of 0.00 - 2.00. Variables 1 and 4 in this table pertain most directly to the hypotheses stated earlier.

Table 1. Measures Derived from Conflict Data.

	Accuracy	
1.	$\lvert J - Y \rvert$	Accuracy of joint decision
2.	$\dfrac{\lvert S_i - Y \rvert}{\lvert T_i - Y \rvert}$	Overt accuracy (adaptation)
3.	$\dfrac{\lvert S^1_i - Y \rvert}{\lvert T_i - Y \rvert}$	Covert accuracy (adaptation)
	Conflict	
4.	$\dfrac{\lvert S_1 - S_2 \rvert}{\lvert T_1 - T_2 \rvert}$	Overt conflict
5.	$\dfrac{\lvert S^1_1 - S^1_2 \rvert}{\lvert T_1 - T_2 \rvert}$	Covert conflict
	Compromise	
6.	$\dfrac{\lvert S_i - J \rvert}{\lvert S_1 - S_2 \rvert}$	Compromise with independent judgment
7.	$\dfrac{\lvert T_i - J \rvert}{\lvert T_1 - T_2 \rvert}$	Compromise with original training

Subjects

Introductory psychology students (40 males and 40 females) were randomly assigned to four groups of subject-pairs: Male-male (MM), male-female (MF), female-male (FM), and female-female (FF). The male-female and female-male groups differed in that the first member of each pair was trained on the linear cue ("free elections"), whereas the second was trained on the nonlinear cue ("state control"). Eleven further pairs of *S*s were trained but rejected when the nonlinear member failed to meet the criterion within 80 trials.

Procedure

Written instructions were supplied to *S*s, describing the purpose of the study, what they would be asked to do, and the nature of the training and of judgmental policies. The *S*s were not told that their judgments *could not* be perfectly accurate; otherwise, the explanations were as honest and accurate as possible.

Instructions for the training phase indicated that *S*s would be presented with practice problems to "give you some experience with a certain kind of foreign policy that has actually been employed at certain times. Then you will be given an opportunity to put this policy to work by making some decisions about some real problems. . . . *One of the conditions is by far more important than the other, and you should weight one of the conditions much more heavily than the other.*"

Written instructions for the test phase stressed that *S*s would be dealing with situations "in the real world. . . . Since these are real cases they are fairly complex, and your public decisions may differ." *S*s were encouraged to ask *E* for clarification of the instructions at all points, but this clarification was generally restricted to repetition of relevant portions of the instructions.

The training for each *S* proceeded for 60 or 80 trials. The test series followed immediately after training.

Data Analyses

Since the basic unit of analysis for this study was the *pair*, rather than the individual *S*, certain restrictions had to be imposed on the data analyses. Where the derived measure represented the pair as a unit (as in joint accuracy, overt conflict, and covert conflict) a 2x2x10 factorial design with repeated measures was used involving 2 levels of sex of the linear *S*, 2 levels of sex of the nonlinear *S*, and 10 blocks of 2 trials each.

For all other analyses, where measures were made on individual *S*s, the scores were in part a function of the responses given by the other member of the pair; thus merely adding another dimension to the factorial design (to represent linear and nonlinear training conditions) was not appropriate. Instead, separate 2x2x10 analyses were undertaken for linear and nonlinear *S*s. As a result, direct analyses comparing the performance of linear and nonlinear *S*s could not be made within the present design. Hammond (1967, 1969) has indicated that extensive differences in adaptation to the conflict task, conflict, and compromise can occur between *S*s as a function of these training schedules.

Results

Analysis of the last block of 20 *training* trials for all 80 *S*s indicated that all had developed cue dependencies. For linear *S*s the mean correlation (transformed to Fisher's *z* scores and retransformed to *r*s) of the "free elections" cue with the criterion was .97, with a range of .89 to .99; for the "state control" cue the mean *r* was −.13, with a range of −.22 to −.01. For nonlinear *S*s the mean *r* with "state control" was .95, with a range of .77 to .99; for "free elections" the mean *r* was −.09, with a range of −.28 to +.07. The multiple correlations involving both cues and the criterion ranged from .73 to .99.

The analyses of the conflict (test) data, undertaken for all measures shown in Table 1, indicated a significant *trials* effect for every measure. Where such tests could be made, no significant differences between the male-male group and the American sample of Hammond's (Hammond et al., 1968) international study could be discerned. However, the present sample appeared somewhat less accurate in their overt judgments, particularly over the last 10 trials, than did the earlier *S*s.

Table 2. *Summary Table for the Analysis of Variance for the Measure of the Accuracy of the Joint Decision (│J − Y│)*

Source	Sums of Squares	df	Mean Squares	F
Sex of *S*	.09	1	.09	.04
Sex of partner	13.32	1	13.32	5.26*
Sex of *S* × sex of partner	.04	1	.04	.02
Error term between groups	91.19	36	2.53	−
Blocks	123.56	9	13.73	12.91**
Blocks × sex of *S*	5.22	9	.58	.55
Blocks × sex of partner	4.57	9	.51	.48
Blocks × sex of *S* × sex of partner	4.55	9	.51	.48
Error term within groups	344.56	324	1.06	−

*p ≤ .05
**p ≤ .01

No sex differences, either as main effects or as interactions, were found in any measures except those of Joint Accuracy and Covert Accuracy (linear *S*s). A summary of the analysis of variance for Joint

Accuracy is given in Table 2. Pairs in which the nonlinear S was male (groups MM and FM) were significantly more accurate ($\overline{X}$ - 1.77) than pairs in which the nonlinear S was female (MF and FF; $\overline{X}$ = 2.14). These data are displayed, over trial blocks, in Figure 3.

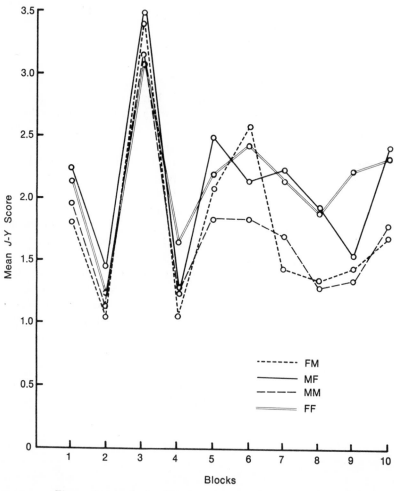

Figure 3. Analysis of the accuracy of the joint decision.

A similar summary of the analysis of variance for the measure of Covert Accuracy, for linearly trained Ss only, is shown in Table 3, where again it is the main effect of Sex of the nonlinearly trained S, which reaches the .01 level of significance. Linearly trained Ss, both male and female, were significantly more accurate in their covert judgments when their nonlinearly trained partner was male ($\overline{X}$=.564) than when the partner was female ($\overline{X}$=.672).

Table 3. Summary Table of the Analysis of Variance for Covert Accuracy $\left(\dfrac{|S - Y|}{|T - Y|} \right)$ for Subjects Trained in the Linear Condition

Source of Variation	Sums of Squares	df	Mean Squares	F
Sex of S	.02	1	.02	.21
Sex of partner	1.16	1	1.16	8.99*
Sex of S × sex of partner	.03	1	.02	.23
Error term between groups	4.68	36	.13	—
Blocks	2.27	9	.25	4.63*
Blocks × sex of S	.10	9	.01	.21
Blocks × sex of partner	.54	9	.06	1.11
Blocks × sex of S × sex of partner	.22	9	.02	.45
Error term within groups	17.63	324	.05	—

*$p < .01$

Discussion

In general, only the first hypothesis of this study could be confirmed. Although the total Canadian sample, whose performance
appeared to parallel that of the U.S. sample, showed a terminal
upswing in conflict more characteristic of Swedish Ss than Americans
(Hammond et al., 1968), there were no significant differences
between the Canadian and U.S. groups on this measure, either in
terms of group effects or group by-trial interactions. Similarly,
although the Canadian Ss appeared somewhat less accurate in their
joint judgments than their American counterparts, these differences
failed to reach customary levels of significance. Generally, then, the
course of conflict reduction and adaptation to the new task appears to
be the same for these subjects as for the Americans and, to some
extent, Europeans. Hammond and Brehmer (1969) have commented
on the great similarity between these Canadian Ss and other groups
from America, Europe, and the Orient that all show highly consistent
patterns of cue utilization and adaptation on a variety of different
measures.

Hypotheses 2 and 3, which called for specific interactions between
the sex of S and blocks of trials on both measures, could not be
confirmed on any of the tests of significance. Nevertheless some low-
level support for these hypotheses may be found in looking at general
trends in the data. For example, on the measure of Overt Conflict, the
FF group generally shows more conflict than any other on each of the
first four blocks of trials and less conflict than any other on the final
four blocks of trials; the MM group, initially at the median on this
measure, shows more conflict than any other on five of the last six
training groups. Similarly, on the measure of Covert Conflict, the FF
groups stand out as the highest in conflict on the first two blocks and
lowest on the last five; the MM group is lowest on the first two blocks

and then emerges markedly higher than any other group on blocks six and seven. Although some of these differences may have been proven to be of statistical significance through use of t-tests on judiciously post hoc selected trial blocks, the absence of significance in the overall F tests suggests that this procedure would be highly inappropriate. These findings can at best be considered as barely suggestive of evidence for these hypotheses.

Hypothesis 4, however, is partially confirmed in the tests of significance provided, in that the FM group is clearly more accurate than the MF group over the last six blocks of trials (see Figure 3) and the effect of sex of nonlinearly trained S emerges clearly from the analysis of Joint Accuracy. Milder evidence at less than customary levels of statistical significance can be found in the analysis of the adaptation of nonlinear Ss: here female Ss actually compromise to the extent of overshooting the criterion on trial blocks five and six. Again, the overall F for this analysis does not reach the .05 level of significance, although the obtained value for sex of nonlinearly trained subjects (4.08) is barely below that required (4.11).

The two significant findings with regard to sex differences revealed in this study appear to be closely related, since in both cases it is the presence in the pair of a nonlinearly trained female S that leads to poorer accuracy. However, since no differences were found in Overt or Covert Accuracy for nonlinear Ss, both males and females seemed equally adept at learning the requirements of the test situation. Apparently, then, the effects of sexuality are most directly felt in the communication phase, preceding Joint and Covert judgments. In the communication phase females who have learned the complex strategy appear unable to communicate it to the linearly trained partner— regardless of that partner's sex—as well as males can. This situation could stem from either an inability on the part of females to *communicate* a complex policy or an unreadiness in Ss, both male and female, to *accept* a complex policy when it is espoused by a female. The lack of sex differences at any other phase of this study suggests that women are as capable as men of learning, understanding, and utilizing complex policies. Thus the second explanation seems more plausible.

Greenstein (1961), in a study dealing with political knowledge in fourth- to eighth-grade children, made two observations: (1) males were better informed about politics than females, and (2) males were sought out for political information by both sexes more often than females were. Since the Ss of the present study were college students, all trained to comparable levels of proficiency, Greenstein's first finding would not appear relevant in this case. However, his second finding appears to be corroborated in the present data, which show that females apparently have no more trouble than males in communicating a simple linear policy but simply *are not believed* when they try to enunciate a complex policy.

The current sexual bias in our society reflects this interpretation. MacBrayer (1960) and Goldberg (1968) found that both males and females tend to see females as less intelligent, less informed, and less able to communicate clearly than males. Goldberg presented his *S*s with identical prose selections on a variety of topics. Half the selections were signed with a fictitious male name ("John T. MacKay") and the other half with a fictitious female name ("Joan T. MacKay"). Even in such areas as dietetics and elementary education, in which women should be more knowledgeable than men, selections "authored" by women were seen as inferior to those (identical) selections ascribed to men; in areas such as law and economics the differences were overwhelming. Goldberg's *S*s were all females.

The absence of any differences beyond this finding of differential credibility appears difficult to explain in view of the extensive evidence for sex differences previously adduced. It is always difficult to interpret nonsignificant results. Yet the fact that a significant Trials effect was found for all measures suggests that those measures were sufficiently sensitive to detect *some* changes. Thus the lack of significance in other comparisons cannot stem from deficiencies in the measurement procedure, such as excessive variability in the data. Possibly the high levels of proficiency brought about by the rigorous training criterion served to obliterate sex differences in cognitive abilities and approaches: of the 11 nonlinearly trained *S*s dropped from the study for failure to meet the criterion, the majority (10) were females. Similarly, the lack of a motivational reward might have blocked the emergence of those sex differences in the management of conflict and compromise that had been found in earlier studies. However, it may also be that sex differences are not quite so pervasive as many researchers have believed.

Stanley L. Singer
Buford Stefflre

Sex Differences in
Job Values and
Desires

E. K. Strong, in connection with his Vocational Interest Inventory, has exhaustively investigated sex differences in vocational choices and interests, but few studies have tried to discern sex differences in job values and desires. The Singer and Stefflre study is one of the few that seriously sets out to determine what women want from employment. It concludes, unsurprisingly, that, whereas men value achievement, women value social considerations.

Strong's (1943) findings, incidentally, generally agree with the results reported here and with common cultural stereotypes. Men prefer mechanical, scientific, physically strenuous, adventuresome, legal, political, military, sales, outdoor, and independent jobs; females prefer musical, artistic, literary, social service, clerical, and teaching jobs. This agreement with stereotypes is to be expected, since most stereotypes are, in fact, quite reasonable. However, in Singer and Stefflre's study the possibility arises that their subjects were responding not according to the way they really felt but according to the way they thought they *ought* to feel. Yet closer observation indicates that this criticism is not valid. The fact that *both* boys and girls chose "Interesting Experience" and "Self-Expression" most often and "Leadership," "Power," and "Fame" least often suggests that the subjects were being reasonably honest and realistic about their hopes and aspirations. (Of course, these findings also imply that sex differences in vocational areas may not be so great as is often assumed.)

The present-day upheaval of traditional sex-typed values and behaviors, particularly among the young, may already have led to marked changes in the variables assessed in this study. Certainly fewer and fewer young women now feel that the role of housewife is sufficient for a life's career, and many males are beginning to question the validity of a life pattern centered around their vocational choice. However, Singer and Stefflre's findings seem also to reflect *contemporary* values: In the mid-1950s the male subjects valued "Self-Expression" over "Leadership" or "Power"; the female subjects valued "Self-Expression" over "Security." Thus, although Singer and Stefflre interpret their data as being consistent with cultural stereotypes, those same data are equally consistent with present-day attempts by Hippies and student activists to replace the old stereotypes with newer, more humanistic expectations.

Personnel and Guidance Journal, 1954, **32**, 483-484. © 1954 by the American Personnel and Guidance Association.

If you had to choose between a job where you could be
job where you could help other people, which would you
having made your choice, would you say that it reflects your real abilities and interests or does it merely conform to the stereotypes that the
world has of your sex?

One of the aspects of self-understanding which may be explored
during vocational counseling consists of the values and desires which
students express with regard to jobs. Centers (1949) did preliminary
work on this problem when he examined the relationships of job
values and desires to socio-economic differences. His major finding
was that the middle class desired a job offering self-expression and the
working class a job offering security. While socio-economic status is
one continuum along which job values may vary, there are other factors which might be expected to affect the wishes which individuals
have with regard to jobs.

Because our culture has varying expectations toward work for the
two sexes, it seemed worth while to examine how the high school boy
differs from the high school girl when responding to the question of
what he really values and desires in a job. In this way we might see if
sex roles do influence adolescent desires in the field of occupational
selection and adjustment.

The present study compared the job values and desires of seven-
teen- and eighteen-year-old Caucasian males with those of a similar
group of females. The sample was composed of 373 male high school
seniors and 416 female high school seniors from the Los Angeles City
Schools who had a terminal vocational guidance program made available to them during the 1952-1953 school year. The steps in the guidance program consisted of: (1) initial structuring meeting during
which the entire counseling program was explained; (2) basic testing
which measured capacity, interest, and temperament; (3) initial interview with a counselor to relate test results and personal-social background to tentative vocational objectives; (4) study of occupational
information; (5) additional testing as needed; (6) final interview to
plan objectives and training; and (7) invitation to the parents to discuss the student's plans with the counselor.

As previously mentioned, Centers has shown that interesting differences in wishes and desires appear between social classes. His technique of learning about people's job desires was to hand them a card
upon which were listed ten different value preferences and to
ask: "If you had a choice of one of these kinds of jobs which would
you choose?" Essentially the same procedure was followed in the
counseling of the high school seniors. During the initial interview the
counselor handed the student the Job Values and Desires Card (see
Figure 1) and asked him to indicate his choice.

Figure 1

Name _____ School _____ Date _____

Job Values and Desires

If you had a choice of one of these kinds of jobs, which would you choose? (Put a number "1" by your FIRST choice. If you have OTHER choices which you would like to indicate, put a number "2" by your second choice and a number "3" by your third.)

—A. A job where you could be a leader.
—B. A very interesting job.
—C. A job where you would be looked upon very highly by your fellow men.
—D. A job where you could be boss.
—E. A job which you were absolutely sure of keeping.
—F. A job where you could express your feelings, ideas, talent, or skill.
—G. A very highly paid job.
—H. A job where you could make a name for yourself—or become famous.
—I. A job where you could help other people.
—J. A job where you could work more or less on your own.

In order to determine whether the observed sex differences were statistically significant, chi square was used with the Yates correction for continuity. Two-by-two tables were established using a male-female dichotomy as one part and each category in the Job Values card against all other categories as the second dichotomy. Example, Rows = (1) Male, (2) Female; Columns = (1) A, (2) non-A.

Table 1 indicates the results of these calculations. Two differences are significant at the 5 per cent level of confidence. With regard to value "B"—A very interesting job—the selection of this category is positively related to being a girl. Another way to express this finding is to say that the desire for a job offering interesting experience is characteristic of girls to a significantly greater extent than it is of boys. The reverse is true for value "J"—A job where you could work more or less on your own—the selection of which is more characteristic of boys than girls.

Three differences are significant at the 1 per cent level of confidence. The selection of value "D"—A job where you could be boss—and value "G"—A very highly paid job—is positively related to being a boy. The desire for—A job where you could help other people—value "I" is characteristic of girls to a significantly greater extent than it is of boys. In summary, a desire for a job offering power, profit, and independence is significantly overselected by the boys, while girls are

Table 1. *Chi Square of Sex Differences in Job Values and Desires.*

Category	Male (N = 373) %	Female (N = 416) %	P
A. Leadership	3	2	
B. Interesting experience	21	28	< .01
C. Esteem	3	3	
D. Power	4	1	< .05
E. Security	13	9	
F. Self-expression	21	25	
G. Profit	12	4	< .05
H. Fame	4	3	
I. Social service	6	18	< .01
J. Independence	13	7	< .01

more inclined to select job values characterized by interesting experiences and social service.

These findings seem to indicate that these students have learned their sex stereotypes very well. The aggressive male is instructed to go out and set the world on fire—be the boss, work on his own, and make lots of money; the submissive girl should strive for an "interesting" job where she can "help other people." This study does not tell us how well these values are translated into actual selection of a vocational objective nor how long these adolescent value patterns survive into adulthood. We do not know if the socio-economic differences found by Centers in adult males on this variable of job values are also present in adolescents. From this study, it is possible only to say that in this sample the indication of job values and desires is significantly related to the sex of the adolescent respondent. Furthermore, the variation in job value preference is compatible with our present more general cultural definition of "maleness" and "femaleness."

Three　　　　Sex-Related Behavior

This final section deals with personality differences between the sexes that seem clearly related to sexuality. Anthropologists and psychologists have speculated and done observational, anecdotal research in this area since the beginning of the 20th century. However, statistical data have been rare, and in most of the reports it is difficult to separate objective fact from personal bias. The preferred method for assessing these differences has been comparison of case histories (which at their best are only more boring than erotic novels). Thus the extensive statistical studies of Kinsey and his coworkers (Kinsey et al., 1948, 1953) and the more recent experimental investigations of Masters and Johnson (1966) are welcome additions to the literature—if only because they prove that this sort of research can indeed be done.

The readings in the section include a trenchant criticism by Barmack of Kinsey's interpretation of his data as they relate to sex differences; a study by Jones and Mussen on the effects of rate of sexual maturation on personality; a pair of studies of sex differences as related to heterosexual behavior and interests; and, finally, an excerpt from an interview with Masters and Johnson, who provide some insights into the possible psychological significance of their work.

Kinsey's and Masters and Johnson's works are the two richest sources of information on differences in sex behaviors. Both reports concluded that (1) the clitoris is a homologue of the penis, (2) the clitoris is primarily responsible for sexual excitation in the female, and (3) under controlled conditions, clitoral stimulation appears to lead to the same amount of sexual excitement in the female that penile stimulation leads to in the male. Thus both studies argue that one of the most basic of sex differences—penile (external) versus vaginal (internal) source of sexual excitement—is illusory. This finding has far-reaching implications, since for centuries man has believed that the personality structures of males are more "aggressive" or "active" or "intrusive" and those of females more "compliant" or "passive" or "receptive" *because of* the anatomical site of their sexual impulses. If what Kinsey and Masters and Johnson maintain is correct, this whole structure falls apart, along with much of our intuitive body of knowledge on sex differences. However, Barmack argues that Kinsey's data fail to document this result at all; numerous other critics have made the same point about Masters and Johnson's study because of the artificiality of their laboratory test conditions. Although laboratory investigations *do* falsify reality, the only counter-technique—recording subjective and intuitive impressions—is even more unreliable.

Jones and Mussen, in the article reprinted in this chapter, attempt a more complex approach than most other studies of sex differences: they focus on the effects of different *rates* of sexual development on personality. They show that differences exist, but they are unable to determine whether they stem from underlying differences in gender and sexual development or from society's differential treatment of the sexes and of the fast or slow developers.

These problems are complicated by the fact that, in statistical terms, the two presumed causes of sex differences—biological sexuality and treatment by society—are highly correlated. Whereas in most other areas of psychology scientists would tend to favor the physiological "cause" over the psychological, here and in the case of race differences such an argument is generally rejected. The only real experimental test of this question would involve taking random samples of male and female infants and treating some of the boys like girls and vice versa. However, it is impossible to do so. What little anecdotal evidence we have from transsexualization operations and the like suggests that at some times, and for some people, biological sexuality seems to outweigh social treatment; at other times, and for other people, the reverse is true. Such evidence does not really advance our body of knowledge.

Joseph E. Barmack

Sexual Behavior in the Human Female: Part II. The Biological Data

Barmack's criticism of the Kinsey Report was part of a special book review for the *Psychological Bulletin*, one of the most highly esteemed psychological journals. (Also included was a review by Herbert Hyman of the methodological aspects of the study, but it is of interest primarily to fellow researchers.) Barmack attacked Kinsey et al. for their conceptions of "psychology" and of adequate measures of sexuality. The Kinsey Report on males was also criticized from a psychological standpoint by Terman (1948). These three reviews indicate that, whatever virtues the Kinsey Reports may have possessed (and these are numerous just in the area of the social change they have provoked), psychologists are still far from achieving an adequate analysis of the psychology of sexuality.

Kinsey and his associates present in the third and final part of this volume a comparison of the sexual activity of the male and female ". . . to discover some of the basic factors which account for the similarities and the differences between the two sexes" (p. 567).

The comparison is not restricted to the data reported in the first volume and in the earlier sections of the present one. Instead, it also includes supplementary data and a survey of the literature. The survey is selective and interpretive, and it represents the authors' conception of the nature of sex differences rather than a mere identification of what is known in this field. By their laborious and extensive study of one of the most important aspects of human activity, Kinsey, Pomeroy, Martin, and Gebhard have earned the interest of a wide audience in what they have to say about sexual life. Their statements need not be supported by any data, provided that their views are represented as theory, opinion, or conception. However, insofar as they

Excerpted from "Special Review: Sexual Behavior in the Human Female," by Herbert Hyman and Joseph Barmack. *Psychological Bulletin*, 1954, **51**, 418-432. Hyman's portion of the review has been omitted; this selection originally appeared on pages 427-432. © 1954 by the American Psychological Association and reproduced by permission.

claim to have demonstrated the validity of their conceptions, the reader is entitled to question whether or not this is indeed so.

Their writing is skillful and engaging, but their style is more popular than scientific. They overgeneralize from their data. They take cognizance of opposing viewpoints or contradicting data, and then proceed to advance their own viewpoint in complete isolation. A surprising number of important terms remain undefined, e.g., psychological factors, basic sex differences, sexual capacity, and capacity to be conditioned, among others. A lack of conceptual clarity is the consequence. It is necessary to interpret what they mean, since the meaning is often not evident. A good example is the summary statement in their chapter on anatomic factors in sexual response and orgasm.

> In brief, we conclude that the anatomic structures which are most essential to sexual response[1] and orgasm are nearly identical in the human female and male. . . . If females and males differ sexually in any basic way, those differences must originate in some other aspect of the biology or psychology of the two sexes. They do not originate in any of the anatomic structures which have been considered here (p. 593).

The precise meaning of this statement is that the erotic topography of male and female genitalia will not account for the higher reported frequency of orgasm of male volunteers.

The authors have singled out difference in orgasm frequency as the "basic" sex difference. They could have considered other differences as "basic," e.g., gross anatomic differences, differences in degree of aggression, or attitudes toward children. They did not, perhaps because they believed the most valid data they could obtain and interpret were reports about orgasms. Initially, orgasm was represented as the prime criterion of sexual life, but subsequently became identified with all of it.

There are still other difficulties with the authors' account of the basic similarities and differences between the two sexes, and these will be discussed within the context of five main propositions. They propose that: (a) sexual responses depend upon a "basic" anatomy which is essentially the same in the female and the male; (b) the physiological accompaniments of orgasm are (with minor exceptions) basically the same for the two sexes; (c) males are more readily aroused by sexual stimuli because they have been conditioned more frequently than the female; (d) males are more frequently conditioned because certain unidentified structural characteristics of the cerebral cortex give them a greater capacity to be sexually conditioned than the

---

[1]They define sexual response as those physiological changes which lead to orgasm (p. 594).

female; (e) there are sex differences in changes of frequency of orgasm with age, the levels of the 17-ketosteroids correlating with these differences.

They dismiss the contribution of anatomic factors to an understanding of sex differences in orgasm frequency on the basis of the following arguments: (a) the clitoris is the embryological homologue of the penis and is erotically as sensitive; (b) the vagina is relatively insensitive to touch and is therefore erotically unimportant; (c) female homosexuals prefer clitoral stimulation, and they should know what is most stimulating; (d) the preferred female masturbatory technique involves clitoral rather than vaginal stimulation; (e) there is no evidence for sex differences in the distribution of end organs of touch and sensory nerves.

The argument of the embryologic homologue is hardly pertinent. The fact that genital differences are difficult to identify in the embryonic stage is no guarantee that *functional* differences will not emerge at a later stage. The bills of the shrike and the hummingbird are homologous structures, but function in quite different ways.

Their denial of erotic importance to the vagina is based, in part, on a study in which they asked five gynecologists to test the tactile sensitivity of the clitoris and other parts of the genitalia of nearly nine hundred women. The gynecologists used a glass rod applied lightly to test touch sensitivity. According to this study, the vagina appeared relatively insensitive to touch.

The pertinence of such a study hinges on whether the equation of tactile and erotic is acceptable. This equation is questionable for three reasons:

1. Tactile stimulation is always available in clothed males and females without chronic erotic arousal.

2. Even tactile sensitivity may change when genital tissue is engorged by sexual excitement. There is no indication that the gynecological exploration was accompanied by sexual arousal.

3. Subjectively, tactile and erotic sensations are different.

The same data are also used to contradict the view advanced by Freud and others that the processes of maturing psychosexually involve a shift of the location of the dominant erotogenic zone from the clitoris to the vagina. This shift the authors believe to be biologically impossible (p. 584). The submitted evidence has questionable relevance since what is required is an age comparison to determine whether the clitoris remains the dominant erotogenic zone. No age comparison is provided, but rather they cite as additional support the preference for clitoral instead of vaginal stimulation by women engaged in homosexual and masturbatory activities. This type of testimony can only complicate rather than clarify a problem in which the critical independent variable is psychosexual maturity.

Their whole discussion of anatomical differences in the distribution of end organs of touch, of the density of sensory nerves in the penis and clitoris, in the size of the breast, and of other parts of the body has no bearing on an understanding of the sex difference in orgasm count unless these anatomic factors can be shown to affect orgasm-*seeking* behavior differentially. This assumption is implied but not examined.

In view of the authors' belief that the vagina is "of minimum importance in contributing to the erotic responses of the female" (p. 592), and since coitus necessarily involves vaginal stimulation it is curious that they did not conclude that anatomic factors contribute to sex differences in orgasm count.

In discussing the physiology of sexual response and orgasm, they review certain muscular, vascular, and glandular responses before, during, and after orgasm. They base their review on a survey of the literature, references to some of their own interview data, and what is apparently a substantial amount of undocumented personal observation. While cited studies show rises in pulse rate, blood pressure, peripheral blood flow, forced respiration, salivary secretions, general muscular activity, etc. during orgasm, the evidence bearing on sex differences in these responses at the human level is variable and negligible. The authors conclude that female and male are quite alike as far as the data yet show in regard to all of these changes. While the cited physiological accompaniments of orgasm have intrinsic interest, their relevance to orgasm-*seeking* behavior is again assumed and not critically examined.

The sex difference in speed of orgasm receives special consideration as an attribute of physiological response. They state:

There is a longstanding and widespread opinion that the female is slower than the male in her sexual responses and needs more extended stimulation in order to reach orgasm. . . .

Certain it is that many males reach orgasm before their wives do in their marital coitus, and many females experience orgasm in only a portion of their coitus . . . but our analyses now make it appear that this opinion is based on a misinterpretation of the facts (p. 625).

After comparing the speed of masturbation of males and females, they state that ". . . the female is not appreciably slower than the male in her *capacity* [italics mine] to reach orgasm" (p. 626).

Then they conclude: "But because females are less often stimulated by psychological factors, they may not respond as quickly or as continuously as males in socio-sexual relationships" (p. 641).

It is clear from the above that Kinsey and his collaborators are not disputing the existence of differences in speed of sexual response in a heterosexual relationship. Rather, they deny a difference in "capacity" to reach orgasm. Apparently, capacity is what is left after the influence of experience is separated out. This view emerges in the following quotation:

> For instance, the exceedingly rapid responses of certain females who are able to reach orgasm within a matter of seconds from the time they are first stimulated, and the remarkable ability of some females to reach orgasm repeatedly within a short period of time are *capacities* [italics mine] which most other individuals could not conceivably acquire through training, childhood experience or any sort of psychiatric therapy. Similarly, it seems reasonable to believe that at least some of the females who are slower in their responses are not equipped anatomically or physiologically in the same way as those who respond more rapidly (p. 377).

High-speed, high-frequency orgasm apparently represents a constellation of organic qualities which, like germ plasm, are relatively immune to the vicissitudes of experience. However, high-speed, high-frequency orgasm may be given a variety of psychological interpretations including denial of homosexual feelings, feelings of inadequacy, and expressions of guilt or exhibitionism, among others. Accordingly, the review believes it is unwarranted for the authors to dismiss sex differences in speed of response by first separating psychological factors from the performance, and then using speed of masturbation as the metric for sexual "capacity."

Having eliminated anatomical and physiological factors (exclusive of hormones) as an explanation of sex differences in orgasm frequency, the authors then ascribe the main role to psychological factors. Conditioning carries the heuristic burden. Men are more often conditioned by their sexual experience (p. 649). This view is deduced from a sexual comparison of reports of arousal in thirty-three situations. These situations include observing the opposite sex, one's own sex, portrayals of nude figures, own genitalia, etc. In 29 out of 33 of these situations, men reported a higher incidence of arousal than women. It is difficult to assess how many of these reported differences reflect a greater female sensitivity to our restrictive codes on such matters, a sensitivity which may have survived the two-hour interview with the Kinsey staff. For example, consider the four out of thirty-three sets of data in which the sex differences either disappeared or were inverted. A higher incidence of women than men reported arousal from observing moving pictures. The incidence of arousal was about the same for men and women when observing their own sex, reading romantic literature, and when being bitten. These questions appear to the reviewer to be either less loaded for women, or are equally or more heavily loaded for men. For example, to report arousal from observing a nude of the same sex implies an admission of homosexual feelings which would be equally undesirable for both sexes.

Let us assume that the reports are uncontaminated by socially determined sex differences in what is acceptable sexual behavior and treat them as valid data on sex differences in arousal. How do the authors explain the difference? For them to state that the male is conditioned by sexual experience more frequently than the female is no more than a reification of their findings. We need to know why they condition more frequently. Is it due to a socially more tolerant attitude to the male when he seeks such experience? Is he more intensely interested in these experiences? Does his greater aggression lead to a more active expression and gratification of sexual interests? The explanation of Kinsey and his associates does not become obvious until they discuss neural factors in sexual response where the following statement appears:

> Since there are differences in the capacities of female and males to be conditioned by their sexual experience we might expect similar differences in the capacities of females and males to be conditioned by other, non-sexual types of experience. On this point, however, we do not yet have information (p. 712).

Apparently, from the cited statement, the authors believe that the higher frequency of human male sexual conditioning is due to his greater "capacity" to establish an association between substitute and reliable sexual stimuli, and that this capacity might extend to other types of reliable stimuli as well.[2] This explanation (stated as a finding) seems farfetched. It assumes that the male has a greater capacity for associating a class of substitute stimuli which are not peculiar to sex (since almost any stimulus can be associated with sexual response). There is no evidence for an intrinsic superiority of the male in associating in any field.

There are more plausible explanations. The social code for the human female may be more restrictive, she may fear pregnancy, she may not *feel* the need for intercourse as often as the male, the male may be more aggressive—to mention a few. Kinsey and his associates mention these possibilities in one connection or another, but they reject them in favor of their "capacity" theory.

In discussing the locus of the neural mechanisms of sexual response, the authors point out that components of the response pattern, tumescence and ejaculation, are possible without sensation in paraplegics. The organism can thus function at the reflex level via the

---

[2] I am assuming that conditioning is a form of association.

spinal cord without cerebral intervention. But while the sympathetic and parasympathetic nervous systems are also involved in the normal situation, there is no definitive evidence concerning the role of the hypothalamus.

The evidence on the role of the cortex is contradictory. On the one hand, a study on prefrontal lobotomy patients 3.3 years before, and another 3.7 years after psychosurgery, shows no appreciable deviation in orgasm frequency from corresponding normal age and sex groups. On the other hand, the authors refer to data which show that damage to the cerebrum as a whole, and particularly to the cortex, may reduce an animal's capacity to react to psychosexual stimuli. The reduction is directly proportional to the extent of damage to the cortex. In spite of the contradictory evidence, they conclude that "although the data on the relation of the cortex to sexual behavior are limited, they do show that this is the part of the nervous system through which psychosexual stimuli are mediated" (p. 712).

There are few performances indeed which cannot be credited, with equal justification, to the cerebral cortex. The authors find support for their position from the demonstration that the male rat's copulatory behavior (and that of other animals) is more dependent on an intact cortex than that of the female. His performance requires more direction, coordination, and initiative. These differences make the male's copulatory behavior more vulnerable to cortical damage, but it does not follow, even in the rat, that cortical differences are the cause of their sex differences.

The final chapter is more carefully written. In it the authors address themselves to the problems of sex differences in the effects of aging on frequency of orgasm, and whether or not these differences have hormone correlates. Table 1 condenses and reflects the data they provide on age trends.

Table 1. Weekly Frequency of Orgasm from All Causes.

	Age 15	Age 50
Single male	2.3	1.1
Single female	0.5	0.4
	Age 20	Age 50
Married male	3.2	1.3
Married female	2.2	0.8

What hormone changes correlate with these differences? Data on hormone assays were not obtained from Kinsey respondents, but from studies reported in the literature. Estrogen and androgen levels do not correlate with the Kinsey data. The changes of 17-ketosteroid levels with age show a closer relationship, but there are marked deviations in the age range from 15 to 27, making a simple causal relationship untenable.

In addition to the hormones mentioned, they consider the effects of hormones from the pituitary, the thyroid, and others from the adrenals. While the latter may affect sexual behavior, it is largely as a result of their influence on the general metabolic level.

They conclude that no hormone affects sexual preferences, interests, or techniques in a selective way, but may rather modify the general level of sexual activity.

To sum up, the conception of the nature of sex differences which Kinsey and his associates have elaborated is at best awkwardly stated and misleading in many particulars. It would be wise to distinguish sharply between the valuable data that they collected and their interpretation of sex differences. While the authors acknowledge repeatedly the importance of psychological factors in understanding sex differences in orgasm frequency, the constructs that they have made central to their presentation are sexual capacity and conditioning capacity. Since they think of capacity as something devoid of experience, we are left with the question, "What do they mean by psychological?"

Mary C. Jones
Paul H. Mussen

Self-Conceptions, Motivations and Interpersonal Attitudes of Early- and Late-Maturing Girls

One aspect of sex that has been largely overlooked thus far in this text is the effect of sexual maturation on boys and girls at puberty. Jones and Mussen examine this issue directly by comparing projective stories of late- and early-maturing girls and boys. Their data are more meaningful than the usual statements that both boys and girls find these changes upsetting and exciting and respond to them by taking a greater interest in their sexuality.

Jones and Mussen have been associated with the Institute of Human Development of the University of California at Berkeley (the "California Group"), which is rivaled only by the Fels Institute in terms of the wealth of material it has produced on human development from infancy to maturity.

"The changing body and the changing self" is a phrase associated with adolescent development (Zachry, 1940). It suggests that the shaping into mature form of the childhood body pattern is accompanied by new self-concepts. These altered attitudes toward the self reflect at least in part the youth's response to his physical metamorphosis.

What "growing-up" connotes for the individual adolescent depends upon a complex of psychobiological factors. One of the most important of these is rate of physical maturation. Adolescent growth may be relatively regular and even, or it may be uneven or abrupt. The timing of puberty, in relation to social norms of the peer group, may present problems of special importance for some adolescents.

Previous reports of systematic comparisons between the behavior and personality characteristics of early- and late-maturing adolescents have indicated that acceleration in growth tends to carry social advantages for boys (Jones & Bayley, 1950; Mussen & Jones, 1957) but disadvantages for girls (Jones, 1949). At their peak of growth, early maturing girls are not only taller than their girl classmates but are

Child Development, 1958, **29**, 491-501. © 1958 by The Society for Research in Child Development, Inc.

actually taller than most of the boys in their class (Shuttleworth, 1939). They are conspicuously large at a time when physical size is not an asset for girls in our culture. Many girls consider tallness to be a physical stigma (Stolz & Stolz, 1944). At the end of adolescence the early-maturing are no longer taller than their age-mates, but in body proportion they tend to have a broad and stocky build (Shuttleworth, 1937), less attractive (in terms of current feminine standards) than the more slender physique of the late-maturing.

Among boys, ascendance in size and musculature is an asset because of our cultural values and the functional advantages of such a build for athletic prowess. This more favorable status is indicated in observational records for early-maturing boys. Staff members rated them as physically more attractive and better-groomed than the late-maturing, and in social situations they were more poised and matter-of-fact, and less attention-seeking (Jones & Bayley, 1950).

In contrast, both classmates (Tryon, 1939a) and adult observers (Newman, 1946) saw the early-maturing girls relatively submissive, listless or indifferent in social situations, and lacking in poise (Jones, 1949). Such girls have little influence upon the group and seldom attain a high degree of popularity, prestige or leadership (Jones, 1958).

The girls in the slower-maturing classification were seen as relatively more outgoing and more assured. They were eager, animated, peppy, and talkative. This behavior seems to be acceptable among girls since those who exhibit it are also described as confident and having leadership abilities (Jones, 1949). While the same characteristics of expressiveness are attributed to slow-growing boys, it is associated in their case more specifically (and especially in later adolescence) with show-off behavior, affectation, and tenseness (Jones, 1943; Jones & Bayley, 1950).

In accounting for these sex differences in the response to early or late puberty, we may note that although early-maturing boys have physical advantages over other boys and are socially in step with girls, the girl who develops earlier than her classmates may be temporarily isolated. H. E. Jones has expressed this as follows:

> The early-maturing girl quite naturally has interests in boys and in social usages and activities more mature than those of her chronological age group. But the males of her own age are unreceptive, for while she is physiologically a year or two out of step with the girls in her class, she is three or four years out of step with the boys—a vast and terrifying degree of developmental distance (1949, p. 78).

A study of responses to the Thematic Apperception Test, given to members of the Adolescent Growth Study when they were seniors in high school, yielded a somewhat unfavorable psychological picture for the late-maturing boys. Compared with their early-maturing peers, they showed greater evidence of negative self-concepts, prolonged dependency needs, feelings of rejection by others, rebellious attitudes toward parents, and strong affiliative needs. These findings were in agreement with evidence from other sources (Mussen & Jones, 1957).

A similar TAT comparison of early- and late-maturing girls should be expected to show results different from those obtained for boys. Thus, it might be expected that early-maturing girls would reveal negative self-feeling and less satisfactory interpersonal attitudes.

Procedure

The present study, paralleling that for boys, was designed to investigate the relationship between maturational status and self-conceptions, motivations, and interpersonal attitudes in a normal public school sample of girls (Jones, 1940). Personality assessment was made on the basis of their responses to the Thematic Apperception Test (TAT).

The 34 17-year-old girls of this investigation constitute approximately the 20 per cent at each extreme of the total sample of the Adolescent Growth Study, selected on the basis of their physical maturity status as determined by X-rays of the wrists and hands (Bayley, 1943). Sixteen had been among the most consistently accelerated over a four-year period during adolescence; the other 18 were among the most consistently retarded. All of the subjects took the TAT at around 17 when they were seniors in high school.

The TAT consisted of 18 pictures: nine from the Murray set which is now standard (cards 1, 5, 6, 7BM, 10, 11, 14, 15, 17); five pictures from the set generally used in 1938 when these data were collected (a man and woman seated on a park bench; a bearded old man writing in an open book; a thin, sullen, young man standing behind a well-dressed older man; a tea table and two chairs; an abstract drawing of two bearded men); and four cards not in the Murray series (a madonna and child, the nave of a large church, a dramatic view of mountains, a boy gazing at a cross which is wreathed in clouds).

The tests were administered individually. Each card was projected on a screen while the subject told a story which was recorded verbatim. Standard instructions were given for the Murray cards, and subjects were asked to describe the feelings elicited by the other four pictures. Most of the stories were brief.

The scoring scheme involved counting the relevant needs, press, and descriptions of the heroes of the stories, the assumption being that the storyteller has identified with the hero; the hero's needs are the same as the girl's; the press that impinge upon the hero are the ones that affect the girl telling the story. A total of 20 needs, press, and descriptive categories, each defined as specifically as possible, was

Table 1. Number of Early- and Late-Maturers Scoring High in TAT Variables.

TAT Variable (with Definition)	High Early-Maturers	High Late-Maturers	p	p (boys)
Negative characteristics–H is described in negative terms (e.g., imbecile, weakling, fanatic).	3	13	.002	.01
p Dominance 1–H forced by parents to do something he doesn't want to.	2	7	.08	.09
p Dominance 2–H prevented by parents from doing something he wants to.	3	6	–	–
p Dominance 3–Total instances of H's being forced by parents to do something and/or prevented from doing something.	4	10	.07	.11
p Rejection–H rejected, scorned, or disapproved by parents or authorities.	3	7	.21	.03
n Aggression 1–H is aggressive in physical, asocial way.	8	9	–	.02*
n Aggression 2–H is mad at someone, argues.	12	14	–	.10*
n Aggression 3–Total of all H's aggressive actions.	5	8	–	.10*
n Autonomy 1–H leaves home.	8	10	–	.20
n Autonomy 2–H disobeys or defies parents.	4	5	–	.11
n Autonomy 3–Total of instances in which H leaves and/or defies his parents.	5	7	–	.02
n Affiliation 1–H establishes good relations with his parents.	9	8	–	–
n Affiliation 2–H falls in love, has a romance, marries.	11	7	.08	.05*
n Affiliation 3–Total instances in which H establishes and/or maintains friendly relations.	7	6	–	.11*
n Succorance–H feels helpless, seeks aid or sympathy.	5	10	.16	.06
p Nurturance 1–H is helped, encouraged, or given something by parents.	5	7	–	.18
p Nurturance 2–H is helped, encouraged, or given something by someone else (not parents).	5	10	.16	.02
n Achievement–H attempts to attain a high goal or do something creditable.	7	13	.09	–
n Recognition–H seeks fame and/or high prestige status.	3	12	.01	–
Denial of Feelings–S states that picture elicits no thoughts or feelings.	10	9	–	.06

*Differences are in the opposite direction for boys as compared with girls.

developed in the analysis of the protocols. A score for each subject for each TAT category was derived by counting the number of stories in which it appeared. Table 1 presents a list of the categories used, together with definitions of these categories.

To test the reliability of this analysis, one of the authors (PM) and another psychologist[1] independently scored 15 complete protocols (300 stories). The percentage of interrater agreement was 90, computed by the usual formula (number of agreements divided by number of agreements plus number of disagreements).

In order to eliminate bias, the scoring used in the present study was done "blind," that is, independently of knowledge of the subject's maturational status.

Results

Frequency distributions of the scores of all subjects were made for all the TAT variables. Each distribution was then dichotomized at the point which most nearly enabled the placing of half of the 34 subjects above, and half of them below, the dividing point. Subjects having scores above this point were considered high in this particular variable; those with scores below this point were considered low in this variable.

Table 1 lists the TAT variables together with the number of late- and early-maturers with high scores in each variable. The exact probabilities of obtaining these distributions of high and low scores in the two groups (or all other possible more extreme sets), calculated in accordance with Fisher's method (Fisher, 1938), are given in the fourth column. The last column gives the levels of significance of the differences between early- and late-maturing boys on these same variables, previously reported by the authors (Mussen & Jones, 1957).

As may be seen from Table 1, early- and late-maturing boys differed from each other on many more characteristics than the two groups of girls did. The boys' groups were significantly different from each other, at the 5 per cent level or better, in six of the 20 variables scored, while the early- and late-maturing girls differ significantly in only two of the variables (*negative characteristics* and *n Recognition*). It should be noted, however, that the *direction* of the differences tended to be the same, rather than reversed, in the two sets of data. For example, the following similarities may be noted:

1. In this list of characteristics a significantly greater proportion of

[1]We are indebted to Dr. Virginia B. Ware for her participation in this aspect of the study.

late-maturing girls than of early-maturing girls have high scores on *negative characteristics*. This finding is similar to that found in the comparison of early- and late-maturing boys. For girls, it is contrary to expectation.

2. The differences between early- and late-maturing girls in respect to *p Dominance* and *p Rejection* are similar to those for early- and late-maturing boys in these variables. These may be interpreted to indicate slightly poorer parent-child relationships among the late-maturing.

3. The early- and late-maturing boys differ significantly on *n Autonomy 1*, suggesting a greater tendency for the late-maturing to avoid or defy authority. The differences are in the same direction for girls, but are not significant.

4. Similar results for boys and girls in *n Succorance* may be interpreted as showing some tendency for stronger dependency needs in the late-maturing.

5. Similar results for boys and girls in *p Nurturance* (significant in one variable for boys) may also be interpreted as indirect indications of stronger dependency needs in the late-maturing.

The chief differences between the sexes are as follows:

1. With respect to *n Aggression* more early- than late-maturing girls show "argumentative aggression," but the two groups of girls do not differ in physical aggression. On the other hand, more early-maturing than late-maturing boys show high degrees of both kinds of aggression.

2. On one category of *n Affiliation* (involving romantic love) higher proportions of high scores are shown for early-maturing girls as contrasted with their late-maturing peers. The differences between the early-maturing and the late-maturing boys are in the opposite direction for this category.

3. The variables *n Achievement* and *n Recognition* do not differentiate the two groups of boys. Among girls scores are higher for the late-maturing, very significantly so in the case of *n Recognition*.

4. *Denial of feeling* does not differentiate early- and late-maturing girls but tends to yield higher scores for early-maturing boys.

Discussion

The failure of the TAT data to support observational findings, especially with reference to the variable, negative characteristics, might be accounted for in a number of ways. Some writers report that in many cases thematic fantasies and manifest behavior operate independently and are even negatively related (Mussen & Naylor, 1954). If we assume this to be the case for our subjects, no further explanation would be needed. But there is also evidence from the literature that, for some groups, TAT findings and overt behavior may be congruent (Harrison, 1951). Our data on boys are in line with this assumption, since, according to observational ratings, late-maturing boys tend to be socially disadvantaged, and, according to the TAT, personally more maladjusted.

The findings for girls are quite different, however. The early-maturing received more unfavorable ratings from both peers and adult observers on many characteristics. But in the TAT they appear to be somewhat better adjusted than their late-maturing peers. This discrepancy between observers' ratings and the picture derived from the personality tests may stem partly from the fact that the reported observational records represented an average of repeated ratings taken over a period of time (from 11 to 17 years) while the TAT stories were collected at the end of this period.

Girls who enter puberty early would be expected to have more difficulties in personal-social relations when they are out of phase with their group. However, after the peer group "catches up," these difficulties would be reduced. By the end of senior high school maturational discrepancies, and social distance due to this factor, would be less marked. It is also possible that even a slight improvement in status would bolster morale and be reflected in a projective technique designed to register attitudes and self-concepts.

There is some slight evidence of a trend toward improved social status for the early-maturing in observational ratings over the seven-year period. Twenty-five items concerned with appearance, emotional tone, social participation, responsiveness, and assurance were used in the comparison. Three of these reflected an improved status at the twelfth grade level for early-maturing girls (Everett, 1943). In two of these, "laughing" vs. "sober" and "sociable" vs. "unsociable," the accelerated girls, while still rated lower than the late-maturing, had improved sufficiently so that the differences between the two groups were no longer significant. But for one important characteristic, "popular" vs. "unpopular," the average ratings for the accelerated girls were now actually slightly higher than for the late-maturing, though the differences were not significant. This last year at high school was the only period when the early-maturing girls were rated by observers as above average in popularity.

It is conceivable that other improvements in social relationships were undetected because of the "halo effect" which, in spite of precautions, may have influenced observers who had rated these same adolescents in earlier years. It is not unlikely that if these girls of more mature status had been observed in social groups of their own choosing (presumably outside of school) the behavior picture might have been more favorable.

It may be noted that over the seven-year period the observational records received little corroboration from a self-report inventory (Tryon, 1939b). Although differences were not consistent in all categories, the early-maturing girls tended to score more favorably than the slow-maturing on "total adjustment," and also on family adjustment and feelings of personal adequacy. These data from the self-report inventory seem to be generally consistent with the findings from the TAT.

However, we may note that in both the inventory and the TAT the early-maturing girls appear in a somewhat better light than in their reputation scores or in ratings by adult observers. In some individual cases a favorable self-report score should not be taken at face value, in view of the tendency for some individuals to cover up or deny their deficiencies.

The only other variable which yields a significant difference between the maturity groups is the category n Recognition, late-maturing girls manifesting a greater desire for personal recognition. The results for n Achievement, though not showing significant differences, tend to support these findings. Other data for this group of girls would lead us to expect this relationship between maturity status and desire for recognition. Late-maturing girls were rated by adult observers as attaining higher prestige, showing more leadership, and having greater stimulus value than their early-maturing peers (Jones, 1949). They were also mentioned more frequently in the high school daily paper over a three-year period and were elected to more offices in extra-curricular activities (Jones, 1958). The late-maturing girls' leadership abilities, their greater social participation, and their apparent social success may have been more closely related to desires for recognition and achievement in the social sphere than to a need for affiliation (Jones, 1958).

It should be noted that, among boys, n Achievement and n Recognition were not significantly associated with rate of physical maturation. Perhaps this is due to the fact that for boys in our culture the pressures to strive for achievement and personal recognition are powerful and pervasive; hence, the boy's physical status may have little influence on his acquisition of strong achievement and recognition needs. Since these cultural pressures are undoubtedly less severe for girls, the strength of these personal needs may be more influenced by such factors as rate of physical maturation.

As we have pointed out in an earlier article (Mussen & Jones, 1957), the relationship between physical status and psychological characteristics in boys is by no means simple. The evidence of the present study indicates that this relationship is even more complex in the case of girls. While the TAT analysis reported in this study suggests that early-maturing girls have fewer negative self-concepts and fewer needs for personal recognition, the results must be interpreted very cautiously. Since only two variables were found to be significantly related to physical status, it is obvious that many psychological and social factors are more important than rate of maturing in determining girls' self-concepts and personality characteristics. Furthermore, these data, considered together with the data from earlier studies on girls (Jones, 1949; Jones, 1958), suggest that the rate of maturation may affect overt behavior and covert characteristics in different—sometimes seemingly contradictory—ways.

It is also possible that, at least for girls, early- or late-maturing means different things at different stages of adolescent development. It has been proposed that since girls who enter puberty early are out of step physically with both the boys and girls in their classrooms, they tend to be socially handicapped during early adolescence. We have assumed that this would carry emotional hazards, and evidence is available from observational data and reputation measures to indicate that this is the case (Jones, 1949).

However, the accelerated girl may gain assurance from knowing that she is on the way toward a goal which is a common task for all adolescents, that of being an adult. By the end of high school, many girls in this group were beginning to feel that they had made satisfactory progress toward this goal. If, in addition to this, she can cope with the problems of this period without too much stress, her self-esteem and feelings of adequacy may be enhanced. A resulting improvement in self-concepts may be reflected in the relative infrequency of negative characteristics in TAT stories.

In conclusion, it is evident that each individual's unique personality structure is determined by a complex of interacting variables, including rate of maturation. Comments made by these subjects as young adults indicate that they were aware of a variety of surface phenomena which affected their adolescent adjustment:

"High school is not a pleasant memory. I felt remote from my mother. If I could have talked to her, it would have helped" (a slow-maturer).

"I wasn't very happy in adolescence. My father was out of work. I felt inferior outside my own circle of friends—I always aimed to please" (a very popular late-maturing girl).

"I was slightly rattle-brained" (a popular late-maturing girl).

"I didn't have much fun in high school. I look forward to more happiness now than I did when I was in high school. I was an ugly duckling" (a slow-maturer who ascribed many negative characteristics to the hero).

"I seemed to be separated from friends in high school. I'm more outgoing now, less cautious and fearful" (accelerated girl).

"I was overweight and sensitive about it—now I take things more for granted" (accelerated girl).

"I had a feeling of being different when growing up" (accelerated).

"I felt stupid in school" (accelerated girl).

"I was very lacking in self-confidence in high school" (accelerated girl).

"I'm more optimistic now. I didn't know many people in high school. I would make an effort to get on with people if I had it to do over again" (accelerated).

Feelings of inadequacy and isolation are expressed by these girls and they are attributed to lack of mental ability, financial difficulties, separation from parents, poor social status, overweight, and unattractiveness. They are about equally common among those whose maturational status was at one extreme or the other.

It is obvious that the findings for this specific group of girls need to be particularized for each individual. These results might be modified also for girls in another geographical area or social level or in another generation. It is possible that school and community programs may be able to de-emphasize maturational status by providing an easier access to mixed social groups through classroom, extra-curricular, and recreational activities which cut across age classifications.

Summary

The present study was designed to investigate the relationship between maturational status and TAT scores for a group of physically-accelerated as contrasted with a group of slow-developing girls from a normal classroom sample. The TAT protocols of 34 17-year-old girls—16 who had been consistently accelerated and 18 who had been consistently retarded—were analyzed according to a scoring scheme involving 20 needs, press, and descriptive categories.

The scores of early- and late-maturing in each of the categories were compared. Earlier reports (Jones, 1949; Jones, 1958) had indicated that girls who reach puberty early are likely to be socially disadvantaged, at least until the rest of their age group "catch up" with them. It was assumed that this social disadvantage would be reflected in the TAT protocols and that differences between the two maturity groups in self-concepts, attitudes, and motivations would be found. Analysis of the data of the present study found few striking differences between the two groups of girls. However, early-maturing girls had significantly lower scores on the category *negative characteristics*, indicating more favorable self-concepts. This finding is contrary to what might have been expected on the basis of observational ratings by adults and reputational ratings by classmates. On the other hand, the TAT results are in line with scores (total adjustment, self-adequacy, family adjustment) on a self-report inventory.

Late-maturing girls have significantly higher scores on *n Recognition*, which is corroborated by data from other sources.

When the differences between early- and late-maturing girls are compared with the differences between early- and late-maturing boys (Mussen & Jones, 1957), they are found to be in the same direction more often than in the opposite. These findings are interpreted to indicate that late-maturing adolescents of both sexes are characterized by less adequate self-concepts, slightly poorer parent-child relationships, and some tendency for stronger dependency needs.

It has been emphasized that complex psychological and cultural factors as well as maturational status contribute to personality development and that the pattern of these influences varies for each individual.

Robert H. Coombs
William F. Kenkel

Sex Differences in Dating Aspirations and Satisfaction with Computer-Selected Partners

The increasing prevalence of blind dating arranged by computers has raised a host of quasi-moral and personal questions. Clearly, if respondents to the computer questionnaires are frank and honest in their responses, and if the questionnaire items are selected to tap relevant areas of compatibility, computer selection can greatly increase one's chances of finding a suitable partner for an evening—or a lifetime. However, both these "ifs" are still uncertain, and proponents of computer-matching techniques are pushing ahead in their zeal to aid compatibility (and make money) at a rate some-what in excess of what knowledge of the variables might indicate. Moreover, computer matching appears contrived, artificial, and mechanical —characteristics that are alien to the kind of romantic, individualistic love that these matching procedures implicitly or explicitly attempt to promote.

Coombs and Kenkel examine some differences between the sexes in terms of aspirations and satisfactions with computer-selected partners. Their results substantiate what intuitive expectations would lead one to anticipate.

The structural-functional views of Talcott Parsons are used as the rationale for predicting sex differences in dating aspirations and partner satisfaction. Blind dates were arranged for 500 male and 500 female students by an I.B.M. computer. Evidence was found to support the hypotheses that (1) women would have higher aspirations for a dating partner, in the sense of more socially desired characteristics, than would men; and that (2) women would register a high degree of satisfaction less frequently than men following the first date. The findings are compared with popular notions of male-female tendencies for romantic love at first acquaintance.

If several hundred young men and women were asked about the qualities they consider desirable in a dating partner, we would expect to discover a variety of responses. If these same people were then paired off as dating partners on the basis of their responses, we would anticipate that some would be better pleased than others with their

Journal of Marriage and the Family, 1966, **28**, 62-66.

blind dates. While variation in dating aspirations and in satisfactions with a dating partner would normally be expected, a sociologist would expect also to discover some regularities with regard to both phenomena. It is the purpose of this paper to show why we should predict that there are sex-linked differences with regard to characteristics desired in a dating partner and with respect to satisfaction with one's blind date. It is the further purpose to test such predictions with data from over 300 couples in a situation similar to that described in the opening sentences of this paragraph.

The structural-functional views of Talcott Parsons (1959) are used as the basic rationale for predicting sex differences in dating aspirations and satisfactions. He views the American family in a state of balance and integration with the rest of the social structure, notably the occupational structure. Since family status is largely determined by the income and prestige level of the husband's occupation, the masculine role is firmly anchored in this occupational structure. A boy soon learns that the only way to become a real man in our society is to have a good job and to earn an adequate living. However, the dominant adult female role, particularly among middle-class families, is that of housewife and mother. Structurally, the importance of this sex role differentiation, aside from providing household and children care, is the shielding of the wife from competition in the occupational sphere, thus fostering a feeling of self-respect for the breadwinner and harmony for the family unit. Because of this structural situation, a girl's adult security depends to a large degree on her relation to the one particular man she marries. Since to so large a degree the meeting of her social, economic, and personality needs depends on this one, almost irrevocable decision, she is apt to be more serious-minded about the processes involved in mate selection. If she chooses wisely, the life chances for her and her children are greatly enhanced.

The differential implications of mate selection suggest that, when asked about the characteristics they desire in a dating partner, women will exhibit higher, in the sense of more socially desirable, standards than men. In listing the qualities desired in a dating partner, we would therefore hypothesize that college women, more than college men, would consider important those traits that are both judged desirable in the social system of the campus and portend of success and high approval in the larger society (Hypothesis 1).

In everyday language, women would be expected to show interest in a "good prospect." But it takes time to analyze a man's occupational potential and role capabilities, especially since the average age for marriage is such that the occupational prospects of a suitor are usually still indefinite. This suggests, then, that women will exhibit a greater degree of caution with respect to their evaluations of a dating partner. In terms of the present study, we would therefore anticipate that women would give more guarded responses regarding their impressions of the men they were dating for the first time. We would hypothesize that women, less frequently than men, would register a high degree of satisfaction following the first date (Hypothesis 2).

Method

A unique situation arose for testing the hypotheses derived from structural-functional theory that there exists a sex differential with respect to dating aspirations and satisfactions with a dating partner. This was a special campus dance in which students were paired by use of an I.B.M. 7074 computer.[1] Prior to the dance, 500 college men and 500 college women completed a questionnaire giving background information on themselves and stating the qualities they desired in a dating partner.[2] Inasmuch as the students realized that their date for the evening was to be selected on the basis of their questionnaire responses, it is thought that they were as honest as possible regarding the characteristics they hoped for in a dating partner.

Information on the students' satisfaction with their machine-selected partners was ascertained through two follow-up questionnaires, one administered shortly after the dance, the other six months later. Six-hundred-and-eighteen persons (307 male and 311 female) responded to the first follow-up study, and 500 (235 male and 265 female) to the second study.[3] Students who did not respond to at least one of the follow-up studies were dropped from the study. This

[1]Only a very few of the participants were personally acquainted prior to the event—2.6 percent knew one another slightly and 0.8 percent were well acquainted. The method of matching couples basically consisted of computing "difference scores" for each boy with each girl. The lower the difference score for a given pair, the more likely they were to be selected as partners. The matching system was based on the relationship of male's and female's aspirations, characteristics, etc., and this did not result in one sex or the other being more likely to get the kind of partner requested.

[2]Male and female participants did not differ significantly with regard to social class background. A near equal proportion of both sexes were from middle-class (white-collar), working-class (blue-collar), and farming families.

[3]The discrepancy between this number (618) and the original 1,000 participants is due to the fact that 121 persons (76 girls and 45 men) did not appear at the event. Thus the number of participants was reduced to 879 persons (424 girls and 455 men). Those whose prearranged partners did not appear were randomly matched with another partner whose identification number differed from our records. Consequently, their follow-up replies were discarded. About 14 percent of the successfully matched persons failed to respond to the first follow-up study. No difference in social background was found to exist between them and the respondents. The response to the second follow-up study was hampered by student mobility during the interim (graduation, etc.).

left a total of 734 persons (368 male and 366 female) who completed the original questionnaire and one or both of the follow-up questionnaires. The data from all three questionnaires were coded and punched onto I.B.M. cards. The Chi-square technique was utilized for testing the differences reported in the present study for statistical significance.

Findings

Marked differences were discovered between the dating aspirations of males and females (Hypothesis 1). In general, the girls had more rigid standards for their computer-arranged partners than did the men. As shown in Table 1, on seven of the eight measures utilized, the female participants specified higher hopes for their partners than did their male counterparts. When asked, "How important is it to you that your date be of the same race as you?" 72.9 percent of the girls answered, "Absolutely necessary," as compared with 56.3 percent of the men. The others replied, "Not necessary but I would prefer it" (23.6 percent female and 34.2 male), or, "It makes little difference to me" (3.5 percent female and 9.5 percent male). These differences were significant at the .001 level. Similarly, when asked, "How important is it to you that your date be a member of the same religion?" the girls took a less carefree attitude than did the men. Among the former, 24.1 percent replied, "Absolutely necessary," while 50.8 percent said, "Not necessary but I would prefer it," and 25.1 percent answered, "It makes little difference." By comparison, the percentages for the male participants were 13.9, 44.3, and 41.8 respectively ($p<.001$).

Girls, more often than men, preferred partners with above average scholastic ability—86.3 percent of the former as compared with 74.4 percent of the latter stating such a preference. The remainder pre-

Table 1. *Sex Differences in Aspirations for a Dating Partner.*

Qualities Hoped for in Dating Partner	Sex with More Pronounced Preference	Chi-Square Value (x^2)	Significance Level (p)
Physical attractiveness	Male	54.08	.001
Same race	Female	28.98	.001
Same religion	Female	26.98	.001
Good dancing ability	Female	25.52	.001
High campus status	Female	25.26	.001
High scholastic ability	Female	16.47	.001
Stylish clothes	Female	12.51	.01
Fraternal membership	Female	7.61	.05

ferred a person with an average scholastic record—13.7 percent of the girls and 25.6 percent of the men ($p<.001$). Similarly, girls more often hoped for a partner with high campus status. The results showed that 16.5 percent of the girls as compared with 5.5 percent of the men preferred a "big wheel" or a "relatively important person," whereas 49.3 percent of the girls and 61.4 percent of the men said that they would be content with an "average" or an "unknown person." The remaining persons (33.1 percent male and 34.2 percent female) expressed no preference ($p<.001$). Although the largest percentage of both male (78.5 percent) and female (76.0 percent) participants had no preference with regard to their partner's fraternal status on campus, more girls (10.1 percent) than men (4.9 percent) preferred a member of a fraternal organization. Among the men, 16.6 percent, and among the girls, 13.9 percent preferred that their partners be unaffiliated ($p<.05$).

When asked, "How important is it that your date wear stylish clothes?" 73.8 percent of the girls replied, "Very important" or "Relatively important" as compared with 64.2 percent of the men. On the other hand, 35.8 percent of the men as compared with 26.2 percent of the girls replied, "Not very important" or "Unimportant" ($p<.01$). Girls also tended to rate dancing ability higher than did men. It was found that 55.2 percent of the former as compared with 37.2 percent of the latter wanted someone who could dance exceptionally well or better than average, whereas 62.8 percent of the men and 44.8 percent of the girls preferred a person with average or below average dancing ability ($p<.001$).

The only quality regarding which men had higher aspirations than girls was that of physical attractiveness. When asked, "To what extent is it important that your date be good-looking or attractive?" 21.5 percent of the men as compared to only 6.6 percent of the girls answered, "Very important," while 23.5 percent of the girls and only 8.6 percent of the men replied, "Unimportant." An equal proportion (69.8 percent) responded, "Reasonably important" ($p<.001$).

The findings also support the view that members of the fairer sex are not as prone toward romantic involvement in a dating situation as are men, nor are they otherwise as easily pleased with their partners (Hypothesis 2). With regard to romantic attraction, the largest percentage of girls (51.6 percent as compared to 37.8 percent of the men) reported, "Absolutely no romantic attraction at all" for their dating partner. Men were more prone to experience a strong feeling of attraction—(18.6 percent as compared to only 7.4 percent of the girls). Approximately an equal percentage (43.6 female and 41.0 male) felt only a slight attraction for their partners ($p<.001$).

Table 2. Sex Differences Regarding Satisfaction with Computer-Selected Partner.

Measures of Satisfaction with Partner	Sex More Frequently Satisfied	Chi- Square Value (x^2)	Significance Level (p)
How much romantic attraction did you feel?	Male	21.63	.001
Did partner have kind of personality hoped for?	Male	12.92	.01
To what extent do you feel it possible to be happily married to person like partner?	Male	9.14	.02
Was partner as physically attractive as you had hoped?	Male	8.00	.02
Were you proud to be seen with partner?	Male	7.03	.05
Was partner as popular as you had hoped for?	Male	6.90	.05
How successfully do you feel you were matched with partner? (1st follow-up)	Male	6.51	.05
How successfully do you feel you were matched with partner? (2nd follow-up)	Male	11.25	.01
How much would you enjoy additional dates with partner? (1st follow-up)	Male	11.90	.01
How much would you enjoy additional dates with partner? (2nd follow-up)	Male	20.94	.001

Women were less optimistic than men that their computer partners offered potential for marriage. When asked, "To what extent do you feel it would be possible to be happily married to a person whose personality, appearance, and the like were similar to that of your I.B.M. partner?" 49.9 percent of the men and 38.9 percent of the girls thought that it was quite possible, while 16.9 percent of the former and 24.8 percent of the latter stated that it was not possible. The others (33.2 percent male and 36.3, female) were uncertain $(p<.02)$.

Despite the fact that men had expressed much higher aspirations for physical attractiveness than had women, they were more easily pleased with their partner's appearance. When asked, "Was your partner as physically attractive as you had hoped?" 32.1 percent of the men (as compared to 25.0 percent of the girls) replied that she was more attractive than they had expected. On the other hand, 34.0 percent of the girls as compared with 24.3 percent of the men thought their partners were just about what they had expected. Approximately an equal proportion (43.6 percent male and 41.1 percent female) said that their partners were less attractive than they had expected ($p<.02$).

Compared with women, men were more generous in their appraisals of the desirability of their partner's personality and of their popularity standing. With regard to the former trait, 40.4 percent of the men as compared with only 27.0 percent of the girls found their partners to have more pleasing personalities than they had hoped for. However, the largest percentage of females (44.7 percent as compared with 35.2 percent of the men) were disappointed. About one-fourth of the participants (24.4 percent female and 27.3 percent male) found their partners' personalities to be just about as desirable as they had expected ($p<.01$). With regard to popularity standing, most persons (46.9 percent male and 46.2 percent female) reported that their partners were about as popular as they had expected. Girls, however, were less often pleased with their partners than men. The findings show that 35.8 percent of the girls and 27.7 percent of the men found their partner to be less popular than they had expected, while 25.4 percent of the former and 18.0 percent of the latter found them more popular ($p<.05$). When asked, "Were you proud to be seen with your partner?" 41.0 percent of the men as compared to 32.0 percent of the girls replied affirmatively, while 22.0 percent of the men and 29.8 percent of the women answered negatively. The remaining cases (37.0 percent of the males and 38.2 percent of the females) gave an indifferent response ($p<.05$).

The second follow-up study found similar differences between the sexes with regard to their satisfaction with their computer-selected partners. In addition, it was found that the male participant did not lose enthusiasm for his partner as rapidly as did the female. In the first follow-up study, 52.1 percent of the men and 42.8 percent of the girls thought that they were matched quite successfully with their partners, while 25.1 percent of the men and 26.7 percent of the girls thought the pairing was "just so-so." The remainder (22.8 percent of the men and 30.5 percent of the girls) thought that they were matched quite poorly ($p<.05$). When the same question was asked six months later, both sexes were much less enthusiastic but especially the girls—46.0 percent (as compared to 31.1 percent of the men) indicating that their match was quite a poor one. The other participants thought the match was either quite good (20.9 percent of the males and 16.7 percent of the females) or was "just so-so" (48.0 percent of the males and 37.3 percent of the females, $p<.01$).

Shortly after the dance, when asked, "How much would you enjoy additional dates with your I.B.M. partner?" 38.7 percent of the men and 26.3 percent of the girls replied, "A great deal" or "Quite a bit," whereas 26.4 percent of the former said, "Not at all" as compared with 17.4 percent of the latter. The others (43.9 percent of the men and 46.3 percent of the girls) were indifferent ($p<.01$). Six months later, when the same question was asked, only 12.9 percent of the girls answered, "A great deal" or "Quite a bit," as compared with 20.0 percent of the men. Although the percentage of men who replied, "Not at all" remained almost the same as in the earlier follow-up study (18.3 percent), the proportion of girls increased sharply (36.2 percent). Those remaining or becoming indifferent were 61.7 percent of the men and 50.9 percent of the girls ($p<.001$).

Summary and Discussion

This study found that girls tended to have higher aspirations for a dating partner than men, in that the qualities they specified were more in keeping with those found in a match that would meet with high social approval. They more often hoped for a person who was a good student, who was popular, a good dancer, a fraternity member, wore stylish clothes, and who was a member of the same race and religion as they were. The only factor that was not rated higher by girls than by men was physical attractiveness; men were much more enthusiastic about having a "good-looking" partner than were women.

While much has been written about romantic love in our society, little effort has been made to ascertain whether men or women have incorporated more of the so-called "romantic complex." The findings of the present study can be brought to bear on the question of possible sex differentials with respect to the specific romantic notion that it is possible to feel strong attraction for someone of the opposite sex at first meeting.

There is some evidence, largely of an informal sort, that women are generally more romantic than men and presumably, therefore, would be more likely to accept the idea of "love at first sight." Young girls are reported to have "crushes" on boys who scarcely realize that the girls exist, and girls are called "boy crazy" more often than the reciprocal label is attached to boys. At a little older age, girls "fall in love" with movie stars and swoon before popular singers. After marriage, it is women who are said to be distressed if romance diminishes and who, conversely, are pleased with romantic symbols and behavior.

Despite the evidence on the romantic nature of women abounding in our culture, the present data indicate that in a first dating situation, men more often than women experience romantic attraction for their partners.[4] For every measure of partner satisfaction utilized in this study, male participants were more enthusiastic than women. They were more prone to be satisfied with her personality, physical appearance, and popularity standing and to think it possible to be happily married to such a person. More often than girls, they desired additional dates. A six-month follow-up study found that while both sexes had lost much of their enthusiasm for the partner, the drop was particularly pronounced for girls.

Initially, we might be prone to conclude that there is a simple relationship between aspiration, and satisfaction, i.e., the higher the aspiration, the lower the satisfaction. Since girls generally had higher aspirations for a dating partner than men, it could follow that they were less likely to be satisfied. However, this view does not explain *why* women had higher aspiration in the first place, nor does it account for the fact that men, who had higher hopes for a physically attractive partner, were actually more often satisfied with their partners' physical appearance than were women. This would suggest that the relationship between aspiration and satisfaction is not as simple as might be imagined.

A structural-functional view might interpret the sex differences in both qualities desired in a dating partner and in satisfaction with the partner as being due to a structural tie of the family unit to the occupational system. Since the family's socio-economic status is largely determined by the occupational position of the male breadwinner, a woman's status and life chances are greatly determined by the performance of her spouse. Since so much is dependent on the personality of her future husband and his success in the occupational sphere, the woman is likely to be more serious-minded than a man about the whole matter of mate selection and to view dating partners in the broader social context of marriage. Thus it would follow that she will have higher aspirations for a partner even on a first date and will be more rigorous in appraising a partner's merits and potential. Since it takes time to do this accurately and since she cannot afford to err, a girl is more likely to be reserved in her evaluations and in her emotional commitments toward her dating partners.

It could be argued that the woman's role in the courtship process is related to her expressions of satisfaction with a dating partner. That is, whether she is much or little attracted to a man at first meeting, it is the man who will ask or will refrain from asking for a subsequent

---

[4]This is consistent with the findings of Burgess and Wallin (1953) that more engaged men than women recalled feeling attraction at first meeting and with those of Kephart (1961) who discovered that more men than women felt that it was easy to become attracted to the opposite sex.

date. A woman can thus spare herself possible disappointment if she feigns a lack of interest in a particular man or, better yet, if she can convince herself that the matter of a subsequent date is of little importance. The man, on the other hand, is in a better position to pursue those interests that intrigue him, even though he will sometimes be rebuffed. Perhaps he is more willing to admit his initial attraction because he knows that he can at least try to arrange for a second date if he wishes. While the findings of the present study on differential degrees of satisfaction are congruent with the idea of differential control over the dating-courtship situation, this reasoning does not seem adequate for explaining the sex differences in dating aspirations. Again, it might be assumed that the women in the study, as a group, were closer to marriage than were the men, and that this factor in turn gave the women's dating aspirations a more "marriage-oriented" flavor. But this would not necessarily explain the differences exhibited by the sexes with regard to satisfaction with their partners. The differential meaning and importance for the sexes of dating and mate selection derived from the structural-functional views of Parsons, however, seem adequate for explaining both the different expectations for a dating partner and the different degrees of satisfaction registered by the sexes. It should be obvious, however, that this study is not a full test of the Parsonian view and that further research should be undertaken.

Don Spiegel
Steven G. Brodkin
Patricia Keith-Spiegel

Unacceptable Impulses, Anxiety, and the Appreciation of Cartoons

In recent years American society has witnessed a rather dramatic upheaval in public attitudes toward sexual material. Books, pictures, words, and acts that were once considered pornographic or obscene have become, if not wholly accepted, at least widely tolerated throughout society. Consequently, questions that were formerly considered taboo for scientific investigation (such as the physiological correlates of orgasm as studied by Masters and Johnson) have become available for scientific study. Psychological journals frequently contain reports on the physiological accompaniments of observing nudes in *Playboy* magazine or some similar topic. In one of the more clever of these studies, Wiggins, Wiggins, and Conger (1968) showed their subjects a series of silhouettes of nudes differing in breast, hip, and leg dimensions. From the relative preference judgments the researchers were able to delineate types of "bust men," "hip men," and "leg men" that corresponded

fairly closely to the Freudian oral, anal, and phallic character types.*

The study by Spiegel et al. was one of the first to investigate sex differences in the perception of these newly legitimized sexual objects. Through "overtly sexual," "mildly sexual," and "nonsexual" cartoons, they attempted to delineate differential attitudes toward sex. Although the cartoons are not further described in their selection, Spiegel and Keith-Spiegel (personal communication) have provided the following examples: "*Overtly sexual*: A scantily clad woman with nearly bare bosom is leaning on a pool table. Her male partner, trying to sort out the balls from the lady's obvious physical attributes, says, 'You're confusing me, Miss Barlow.' *Mildly sexual*: A used-furniture salesman is showing a bed to a couple and says, 'It was owned by an elderly couple.' *Nonsexual*: These are silly, non-drive-related, nonsense cartoons."

It is reasonable to assume that

Journal of Projective Techniques and Personality Assessment, 1969, **33**, 154-159.

*Wiggins and Wiggins (1969) have subsequently denied that their data support the existence of Freudian types: on more sophisticated analysis, they failed to find any individuals who could be called pure examples of any type. We can only speculate about the nature of character "types." For example, should they be conceived as real people or as dimensions of judgment, attitude, belief, and so on along which people can be ordered? Although Freud wrote as if he believed the former (since the other explanation was unheard of in his day), his constant reminders that there are no "pure" types—that all traits are intercorrelated—suggest that he would now support the latter interpretation.

males and females will differ in their appreciation of or arousability by various kinds of "sexy" material. Kinsey et al. suggested that, whereas men can be sexually aroused by a variety of sex-related materials, such as pornographic literature or pictures, burlesque, graffiti, or dirty jokes, women seem to respond only to romantic sugar-coated literature —and not much to that. However, the results of the present study seem strangely inconclusive in that (1) there *are* differences in males' and females' appreciation of these cartoons, but (2) these differences are *not* really related to any of the other measures employed in the study

(acceptability of impulses, sexual disturbance, sexual guilt). Common sense would tell us that sex differences relating to the differences in appreciation of cartoons *should* be demonstrated in these areas.

Perhaps this inconsistency stems from an attempt to fit people into neat boxes. Even in situations as far removed from real life as our psychological aberrations are, college students may be capable of behaving like individualized and independent humans rather than puppets manipulated by theories. Such situations should be welcome, but they are awfully frustrating to researchers.

Summary: Sexual adjustment measures were used to predict "funniness" ratings of overtly sexual (OS), mildly sexual (MS) and non-sexual (NS) cartoons. Male college students were more anxious, more admitting of unacceptable impulses, more sexually frustrated and more disturbed about sexual expression than female students and gave higher funniness ratings to both OS and MS cartoons. In both sexes a strong positive association was found between anxiety level and admission of unacceptable impulses. In females, perceived funniness of MS cartoons was positively associated with sexual frustration and sexual disturbance. In males, funniness of OS cartoons was positively associated with acceptance of sexual impulses.

The focus of this study[1] was upon sex differences in predictors of affective response to overtly sexual, mildly sexual and non-sexual humor stimuli (cartoons) with non-aggressive themes. Byrne (1957) and Strickland (1959) attempted to experimentally induce sexual arousal in their *S*s and to measure its relationship to subsequent appreciation of cartoons with sexual themes. Strickland found that *S*s appreciated sexual humor after being placed in sexually arousing situations, but Byrne found no such direct relationship. The present study was not concerned with the effects of induced emotional states on subsequent reactions to cartoons. Rather, stable and consistent attitudes toward sexual impulses and sexual behavior were assessed and related to appreciation of cartoon humor. The facets of sexual adjustment chosen for study were: anxiety level, admission of unac-

[1]Gratitude is expressed to the Veterans Administration Western Research Support Center for the multiple regression analysis, and to Marie J. Brady for other statistical calculations and manuscript typing.

ceptable impulses, sexual frustration, guilt feelings associated with the expression of sex impulses, acceptance of sex urges, and sexual irresponsibility.

This study was designed to provide answers to three questions: (1) Will male and female college students respond differently to non-aggressive cartoons with sexual and non-sexual themes? (2) Which variables appear to be most promising as predictors of affective response to cartoons of each variety, and are they the same variables for males and females? and (3) Will the prediction of affective response to cartoons be enhanced by combining predictor variables?

Method

Subjects

The *S*s were 35 males and 35 females ranging in age from 18 to 22 years (mean age 19.3) from lower division psychology courses at a local state college.

Materials

Materials for the predictor variables include: (1) the *unacceptable impulse scale* (high scores reflect impulse denial) from the Spiegel Personality Inventory (Spiegel, 1965), (2) the California *F* scale of right wing authoritarianism (Adorno, Frenkel-Brunswik, Levinson, & Sanford, 1950), (3) nine sentence completion items, four of which dealt explicitly with attitudes toward sex, (4) the manifest anxiety scale (Taylor, 1953), and (5) two cards from the TAT which promote heterosexual themes, viz., cards 4 and 13 MF.

Materials for the criterion variables were 21 cartoons arranged in random order. Three independent judges separated a pool of non-aggressive cartoons into three content categories: (1) overtly sexual (OS) which contained blatant, undisguised sexual content, (2) mildly sexual (MS) which contained disguised or mild sexual connotations, and (3) non-sexual (NS) nonsense cartoons which contained no sexual connotations. The seven cartoons judged funniest in each category, for which there was unanimous agreement regarding content, were selected for the study.

Procedure

*S*s were tested separately and told to follow the directions in each section of the booklet. To assure anonymity, *S*s were told to omit their names from the questionnaires and to place them (unobserved) in a large box with other materials when they were finished. Ss were asked to give honest answers, to work with the materials in the sequence given, to answer every item, and to respond in terms of their present feelings.

Results

An objective scoring system was applied to all tests except the projective materials. For these, two experienced judges were asked to assign four ratings to each S's projective productions. The ratings were based upon careful consideration of responses to both sentence completions and TAT cards. Interrater reliability was sufficiently high to justify combining the ratings of projective materials made by them. Thus, all scores used in the analyses are combined ratings (Rater 1 plus Rater 2). The four dimensions rated included: (1) sexual frustration, (2) guilt over sexual activity, (3) rejection of sexual impulses, and (4) sexual irresponsibility. For each dimension, Ss were assigned a rating from 1 to 7. An overall "sexual disturbance" score was calculated by summing the ratings on the four dimensions. A t test for independent groups was used to test the hypothesis that the mean scores for males and females on predictor and criterion variables were from the same populations of means. As compared to females, males were more anxious and admitted more socially deviant or unacceptable impulses. On the projective tests, there were indications of greater sexual frustration and overall disturbance over sexual matters among males than among females. These differences were significant at $p < .05$. Males also rated overtly sexual and mildly sexual cartoons as funnier than did females. These differences were statistically significant at $p < .01$. Although the following differences were not statistically significant, they bear consideration inasmuch as they are consistent with the other findings. Compared to females, males tended to project more guilt feelings over sexual relations, to be more rejecting of sex impulses, and to feel less concern about distinguishing between socially appropriate and inappropriate sexual expression in various settings (sexual irresponsibility). They also tended to enjoy NS cartoons more than females did.

Table 1 gives the Pearson r values among individual predictor variables for males and females separately as well as the significance levels of the coefficients. As may be seen there are some striking differences between males and females in the interrelationships among predictor variables. For females, authoritarianism was significantly correlated with sexual frustration, guilt associated with expression of sexual impulses, and with sexual responsibility. For males, authoritarianism was not significantly related to other predictor variables.

Table 1. Intercorrelation among Predictor Variables.

Variables	Females (N = 35)							Males (N = 35)						
	B	C	D	E	F	G	H*	B	C	D	E	F	G	H
A Authoritarianism	-17	12	34	44	30	-44	31	-12	17	-17	03	08	-30	-14
B Anxiety		-50	03	-33	-38	27	-04		-37	35	00	-15	-04	07
C Impulse denial			-07	41	28	-41	-07			01	22	19	-15	14
D Frustration				80	61	-32	86				22	41	12	76
E Sexual guilt					61	-42	86					55	-39	65
F Impulse rejection						-41	67						-24	76
G Irresponsibility							-12							14

Note:– With 33 df, an r value of .33 is significant at $p < .05$ and an r value of .42 is significant at $p < .01$.

*H = Sexual disturbance = D + E + F + G.

Manifest anxiety was associated with admission of unacceptable impulses in both males and females, with sexual frustration in males only, and with rejection of sexual impulses only in females. In females only, denial of unacceptable impulses was strongly associated with guilt feelings about sex relations and with sexual responsibility. Denial of unacceptable impulses was not significantly associated with any independent variable in males.

A stepwise multiple regression analysis was done to determine whether a combination of variables would increase ability to predict response to humor stimuli beyond that of variables taken singly. Because of sex differences on both independent and dependent variables, separate analyses were done for males and females. Authoritarianism was excluded from this analysis since it was not significantly correlated with any of the dependent variables. Table 2 gives Pearson coefficients of correlation between single predictor and criterion variables, and multiple correlations for various combinations of predictors with each criterion variable for each sex. Each variable title in the tables reflects the high end of the scoring range. An analysis of variance of the regression was done to test the null hypothesis that the estimate based on the regression sum of squares will differ from that based on the residual sum of squares only because of chance sampling errors. This null hypothesis implies that if the entire population were measured, the correlation of the dependent variables with each independent variable would be zero. Multiple correlation values associated with statistically significant F values are indicated by asterisks

Table 2. *Coefficients of Relationship between Predictor and Criterion Variables Using Single and Combined Predictors.*

	Overt		Mild		Non-Sexual	
Predictor	F	M	F	M	F	M
B Anxiety	17	06	-17	-07	-50**	-05
C Impulse denial	-15	-24	05	04	54**	-09
D Sexual frustration	17	01	33*	11	16	19
E Sexual guilt	09	-01	24	16	25	-07
F Impulse rejection	-05	-39*	10	-13	-22	-06
G Irresponsibility	07	21	09	11	-30	22
H Sexual disturbance	-01	-08	29	12	14	11
B, H	17	11	33	15	51*	12
B, C	18	24	18	11	60**	13
H, C	15	25	30	13	56**	15
B, H, C	18	25	33	18	61**	18
D, E, F, G	28	52*	39	37	34	29

Note:—Pearson *r* values are listed for single predictors; multiple *R* values are listed for combined predictors. Asterisks identify correlations associated with significant *F* values obtained from an analysis of variance of the regression.
*$p \leq .05$
**$p \leq .01$

in Table 2. Since the multiple R is a biased estimate of the multiple correlation in the population, corrected values were computed to provide more probable estimates of population values. These values are not shown since in no instance was there an appreciable increase in predictability over a single variable, and it was thus concluded that single predictors suffice to describe the regression.

As may be seen in Table 2, there were *no* instances in which the same independent variables predicted the dependent or criterion variables for both males and females.

For OS cartoons, none of the independent variables predicted funniness ratings made by females, whereas sexual rejection proved to be negatively related to funniness ratings made by males.

For MS cartoons, none of the variables predicted funniness ratings made by males, whereas sexual frustration was positively related to funniness ratings made by females.

For NS cartoons, none of the independent variables predicted funniness ratings made by males, whereas funniness ratings made by females were negatively related to anxiety and positively related to denial of unacceptable impulses.

Thus, with respect to the questions which this study attempted to answer, we may summarize our main findings as follows: (1) Young college males were more amused than were young college females by overtly and mildly sexual cartoons with non-aggressive themes. (2) Although some promising predictors of funniness ratings of sexual and non-sexual cartoons were found and described for each sex, there was no evidence that a good predictor of response to a given kind of cartoon by males is a good predictor of response by females, and vice versa. (3) The prediction of funniness ratings of cartoons for either sex was not substantially enhanced by a linear combination of the variables used in this study.

Discussion

The fact that males were significantly more anxious than females was surprising in view of previous work with similar student groups (Spiegel, Olivo, & Keith-Spiegel, 1968), in which anxiety was higher for females. Nevertheless, there was no evidence that selective factors were operating since students had no advance knowledge of the nature of the project. Even though males and females differed on several variables, it should be observed that scores for either sex did not indicate very high levels of anxiety or sexual disturbance.

Among the factors which may have influenced the results one may speculate that males and females were differentially affected by the assurance of anonymity. Males may have been more prone to admit feelings that they might otherwise have denied because of social desirability considerations. The anxiety mean score for females was similar to our previous work with students of this age. Thus, if anonymity produced an effect, it was primarily on males, who perhaps are ordinarily more defensive than females about openly admitting characteristics which they regard as weak or undesirable.

On the other hand, since the content of the projective tests and the unacceptable impulse scale involves attitudes about sex relations, score differences between sexes may reflect real differences in anxiety, guilt, etc., related to sexual adjustment. It may be that males are more sexually active at this period in their lives than females and are more disturbed about the expression of sexual impulses.

This study produced no evidence of a substantial relationship between authoritarianism and funniness ratings of cartoons. It might be noted, however, that authoritarianism was significantly associated with sexual responsibility in females, and as earlier noted, it was associated in females with guilt feelings related to sexual activity and with sexual frustration. In view of these results it may seem surprising that authoritarianism was not associated with dislike of sexual cartoons in females.

The multiple R value of .60 for females using anxiety and denial of unacceptable impulses as combined predictors indicates that females who were anxious and who admitted unacceptable impulses often did not find non-sexual, nonsense cartoons funny, whereas non-anxious females who denied unacceptable impulses often found these cartoons funny. Although the reason for this may be far from clear, the finding is consistent with the findings of Doris and Fierman (1956) with sexes combined. Their finding of no difference between high and low anxiety groups with respect to sexual cartoons is also consistent with the zero order correlations in the present study between anxiety and funniness ratings of OS and MS cartoons.

The results of this study indicate that it is inadvisable to combine males and females in a single analysis in studies involving the interrelationships among psychosexual and other variables unless separate analyses have shown no differences between mean scores for the sexes *and* no differences in the interrelationships among the variables. Studies which have not heeded this caution might be reviewed with the understanding that significant results could be present for one sex which are obscured by a combined groups analysis involving the interrelationships among several variables.

William H. Masters
Virginia E. Johnson

Interview
(with Nat Lehrman)
(Excerpt)

Human Sexual Response, Masters and Johnson's best-selling summary of their extensive researches in sexual activity, has become the definitive work in this area. However, it has been challenged on both moral and scientific grounds from a variety of sources. Most of the arguments maintain that Masters and Johnson, by subjecting sexual intercourse to scientific investigation, have in some way dehumanized it (an argument similar to that cited by Barmack in his review of the Kinsey studies). The validity of this criticism can only be tested by examining the psychological concomitants of the subjects' sexual experience both within and outside the laboratory. Masters and Johnson present data on this subject in *Human Sexual Inadequacy* (1970). In the selection that follows, these two researchers, gently prodded by a skillful and informed interviewer, provide a brief course highlighting most of what we know, and identifying most of what we erroneously believe, about human sexual behavior.

Playboy: One of your most widely publicized findings concerns the four phases of sexual response—excitement, plateau, orgasm and resolution. Quoting from your book: "The first or excitement phase of the human cycle of sexual response develops from any source of somatogenic or psychogenic stimulation. The stimulative factor is of major import in establishing sufficient increment of sexual tension to extend the cycle. . . .

"From excitement phase the human male or female enters the second or plateau phase of the sexual cycle, if effective sexual stimulation is continued. In this phase sexual tensions are intensified and subsequently reach the extreme level from which the individual ultimately may move to orgasm. . . .

"The orgasmic phase is limited to those few seconds during which the vasoconcentration [concentration of blood] and myotonia [muscle tension] developed from sexual stimuli are released. This involuntary

Excerpted from an interview with Nat Lehrman in *Playboy*, May 1968, pp. 67-82, 200-202.

climax is reached at any level that represents maximum sexual tension increment for the particular occasion. Subjective (sensual) awareness of orgasm is pelvic in focus, specifically concentrated in the clitoral body, vagina and uterus of the female and in the penis, prostate and seminal vesicles of the male. The human male and female resolve from the height of their orgasmic expressions into the last or resolution phase of the sexual cycle. This involuntary period of tension loss develops as a reverse reaction pattern that returns the individual through plateau and excitement levels to an unstimulated state. . . ."

You were, of course, discussing the cycle in a sexually responsive individual. But what happens to those individuals, particularly females, who don't go through the full cycle to orgasm?

Masters: There are periods of irritability, emotional instability, restlessness, pelvic discomfort, lack of sleep. Combinations of these symptoms may develop in the human female. You see, orgasm is a release point for the congestion of blood in the pelvis. This vaso-congestion—which is the medical term for it—is relieved very rapidly if there is orgasm. If not, the release of vasocongestion is slowed, particularly if the woman has had babies and has enlarged blood vessels in the pelvis. Her period of frustration, irritation and pelvic discomfort may last for hours; sometimes—though rarely—a day or two.

Playboy: How about the male? There is a well-known malady among young men, variously referred to in slang as "blue-balls" or "lover's nuts," in which the male complains of severe pain in the testicles if he is stimulated without reaching orgasm. Is there a similar explanation for this affliction?

Masters: Yes. We've discovered in our experiments that when the male is sexually excited and approaching ejaculation, the testicles increase in size; the average size increase may be as much as 50 percent over the unstimulated norm. A young male who is forced to maintain this degree of local vasocongestion for a period of time—without release—may well develop some pain and tenderness. If he ultimately ejaculates, he never notices the local congestion, but long-standing vasocongestion can certainly be painful. Those males who suffer from long-continued "plateau phase" frustration usually either masturbate or have a nocturnal emission and the ejaculation relieves the congestion that way.

Playboy: You used the term ejaculation, not orgasm. In the male, is there a distinction between the two?

Masters: Male orgasm is actually a two-stage affair. The first stage is identifiable by a sensation of "ejaculatory inevitability." This is when he no longer can control the ejaculation but before he actually has any seminal-fluid emission. This stage of ejaculatory inevitability lasts two to four seconds and is occasioned by contractions of the prostate gland and possibly the seminal vesicles. This reaction pools the seminal fluid in that portion of the urethra that runs through the prostate, just outside the bladder. The remaining part of the male orgasm —that of actual ejaculation—is the expulsion of the seminal fluid throughout the length of the penile urethra by contractions of the penile and urethral musculature. The female orgasm, by contrast, is but a one-stage affair.

Playboy: Did you discover any evidence that women ejaculate?

Masters: We have heard from four women who claimed that, with orgasm, they have an overwhelming release of fluid. But we've never had the opportunity to evaluate these women in the laboratory.

Johnson: There are large numbers of women who have physical manifestations that fit their belief that they ejaculate. The fact that many women urinate under the intensity of an emotional experience may very well be a factor here. But we don't know.

Playboy: You have compiled data bearing on the belief that the size of a man's penis can influence a woman's sexual responsiveness. Would you tell us about it?

Masters: There has long been a myth that penile size relates to male stimulative prowess. We found this not to be true. In the first place, the size of the penis usually has been judged in its flaccid state. In this situation, the penis varies greatly in size. But as it becomes erect, the smaller penis goes through much more of an erective process than does the larger penis. So, at the moment of mounting with full erection, the major differences in flaccid penile size have been remarkably reduced. In addition, the female has the great facility of accommodating the penis, regardless of size, and not expanding the vagina beyond the size sufficient for containment. Vaginal expansion, of course, is purely involuntary and is directed toward accommodation of the particular penis in its erect state.

Johnson: It helps to realize that the vagina is a potential rather than an actual space in its unstimulated state. Actually, the vagina is virtually an infinitely expandable organ. After all, it goes from a collapsed state to a size large enough to accommodate a baby's head.

Masters: Of course, we have been talking about physiological response. Psychologically, if the woman really believes that the larger penis in its flaccid state is going to make a difference when it becomes erect, then for her it might. But the really experienced woman would agree that size doesn't make a crucial difference. There are physical exceptions concerning obstetrical trauma that should be mentioned. Vaginal tears or alterations can result in a chronically distended organ that might have difficulty adjusting to the erect penis, *regardless* of its size.

Playboy: Another penile myth concerns the sexual responsiveness of the circumcised versus the uncircumcised penis. What can you tell us about this?

Masters: The uncircumcised male—and, in some versions of the folklore, the *circumcised* male—is presumed to have a greater tendency toward premature ejaculation, because he can be more easily stimulated. We have no evidence that either presumption is true. Fundamentally, we can't find any differences in reaction time, or sensate focus, between the circumcised and the uncircumcised male.

Playboy: Yet another misconception discussed in your book relates to the controversial Freudian theory about the clitoral versus the vaginal orgasm. Would you elaborate?

Masters: It was Freud's concept that if a woman's response was restricted to the masturbatory, or clitoral, orgasm, then it reflected psychic immaturity. She could be considered a fully responsive, hence mature, woman only if she had orgasm during intercourse—by definition, the vaginal orgasm. In order to delineate between these two types of orgasm, Freud presumed they were entirely separate physiological entities. Our research indicates that this is not the case. Certain clitoral changes occur with stimulation of either the clitoral area or the vaginal area, or from manipulation of the breasts or, for that matter, from simple fantasy. These changes are anatomically and physiologically *identical*, regardless of the source of stimulation. Secondarily, it is physically impossible *not* to stimulate the clitoris during intercourse. And I'm not referring to direct penile-clitoral contact.

Playboy: Didn't Freud speculate that the sexually mature woman has transferred sexual sensation from the clitoris to the vagina?

Masters: Yes, but there is no longer any need to speculate about this, because, as I started to say, the clitoris *is* stimulated during intercourse every time the female responds to a male thrust. This reaction occurs regardless of what position she may be in. You see, with each thrust, the minor labia are pulled down toward the rectum and, in the process, stimulate the shaft of the clitoris. So there is no physiological difference among clitoral orgasm, vaginal orgasm, breast orgasm, or for that matter, orgasm through fantasy. Incidentally, since the publication of the test, we've had the opportunity to evaluate three women who can fantasy to orgasm.

Playboy: Some of your critics think that your work contributes to a general overemphasis of the subject of female orgasm. What's your reply?

Masters: We don't think you can overemphasize the importance of this subject. But it certainly has been belabored out of its proper context. The Sixties could be labeled the decade of orgasmic preoccupation. It's been only in the past seven or eight years that this focus on female orgasm has emerged. Some women are developing a fear of nonperformance as a result of all the public discussion about its importance—particularly discussion not necessarily based on scientific objectivity. You can't read any women's magazine today without finding an article about some form of reproductive biology. It may sell magazines, but it also creates a scare type of philosophy that, in turn, may increase either male or female fears of inadequacy.

Johnson: Orgasmic preoccupation could occur only in a society in which sexuality has been so negated that many women have been unable to move confidently through all this discussion with a foundation of self-knowledge. A woman who has or has had a satisfactory relationship—and is secure in its effectiveness—can skim through the magazine article stressing orgasm or listen to the neighbor lady at the coffee klatch brag, "Oh, we have intercourse eight times a week and I'm orgasmic one hundred percent of the time," and still not feel threatened by this kind of discussion. But someone who lacks personal knowledge can be thrown into pure panic.

Playboy: In your book, you also discussed female multiple orgasm. You wrote, "Women have the response potential of returning to another orgasmic experience from any point in the resolution phase if they submit to the reapplication of effective stimulation." Since multiple orgasm was discussed by Kinsey and earlier by L. M. Terman, what particular significance did you attach to it?

Masters: Apart from several physiologic observations of a technical nature, one of the important things we established—to our own satisfaction, at least—is that the female is *naturally* multiorgasmic. This had not been emphasized before.

Johnson: In spite of Terman and Kinsey, scientifically oriented people still imply that this is a freakish thing.

Playboy: Picking up on the phrase "*naturally* multiorgasmic," do you believe that, all other things being equal, the female should achieve orgasm as easily as the male?

Masters: Yes, indeed. We have nothing to suggest otherwise. It would seem that puritan and Victorian social restraints have destroyed or altered significantly the female's natural responsivity.

Playboy: Another aspect of female sexuality discussed in your text is the notion that the female's sexual response is more diffuse than the male's—that is, that women respond sexually with more of their bodies than do men, whose pleasure seems to be centered in the penis. Would you comment on that?

Johnson: This, too, is probably culturally conditioned. We find that those men who value total expression undergo all the thrill and sensate experience of a total body phenomenon commonly attributed only to the female.

Masters: I think what should be stressed here is that physiologically, the male and the female are incredibly *alike* in sexual response —not different. This is really what we tried to emphasize in the text.

Johnson: If I may be permitted to comment on the larger issue implicit in your question—the fact that so many people of *both* sexes feel sexual pleasure only in the sex organs themselves—this is a manifestation of their rejection of their total sexuality. For example, a lot of women do not respond to breast stimulation because of its implied impropriety. A young person exposed to this type of negation will frequently reject the concept of breast stimulation and/or response. An anesthesia comparable with self-hypnosis is induced. I mention the breasts particularly because this type of negation comes out so dramatically when women reject nursing.

Masters: Yes, and this negation may extend even to the genitals —as with the unresponsive woman who claims she never feels a thing during intercourse, no stimulation whatsoever. She has a certain amount of vaginal anesthesia that we're convinced—as are many others—is psychogenically induced and relates to attitude, circumstance and environment. I do want to stress, however, that we lack definitive data concerning the psychological deterrents to sexual response and sexual tension.

Playboy: You use the phrase "sexual tension" frequently in your book. Would you define it?

Masters: Sexual tension is the physiological concomitant to, and reflection of, elevation in an individual's psychic sex interest, expressed in increased blood concentration and muscle tension.

Johnson: If that seems formidable, try to think of it as what the body does in response to sexual interest.

Playboy: Does this tension differ in any way from what is usually referred to as the sex drive?

Johnson: Sex drive has become such a general term that it doesn't have a precise scientific meaning. It's often used to mean the basic drive to reproduce.

Playboy: Can sexual tension be suppressed or denied?

Johnson: It can be denied and it can be displaced—that is, expressed in a nonsexual way. Most likely, if suppressed, it will be expressed involuntarily, through nocturnal emissions and erections or pelvic vasocongestion and vaginal lubrication. These cannot be put aside.

Playboy: Do women experience anything analogous to the male nocturnal emission?

Masters: We have done no dream research, but we're certain that the female can be orgasmic in dreams.

Johnson: And there have been frequent reports of an increase in the volume of erotic dreaming by women who have been abstaining from sex.

Masters: Returning to your question about sexual denial, I'd like to add that sexual demand seems to be a unique physiological entity. Unlike other demands, it can be withdrawn from; it can be delayed or postponed indefinitely. You can't do this with bowel function or cardiac or respiratory function. Perhaps because it can be influenced in this unique manner, sex has been pulled out of context. Lawyers and legislators have taken a hand in telling us how to regulate sexual activity. They don't, of course, presume to regulate heart rate; but, as I say, sexual demand can be denied, even on a lifetime basis.

Playboy: With no ill effects?

Masters: That depends. We've already talked about irritability and pelvic discomfort that can result from not fulfilling sexual demand, but these effects are only temporary. On a long-term basis, many different types of neurosis can develop from continued suppression of sexual tension. But not always; there must be countless lifetime celibates who have not become neurotic.

Playboy: What role do such psychological factors as fantasy and imagination play in enhancing sexual response for either sex?

Johnson: It depends on how you define those terms. What some people call imagination could be described as recall. The only psychological constant in sexual response is the memory of, or the conditioned response to, the pleasure of sensation—in other words, to those things that have become sexually endowed for that person. These may be deliberately invoked during masturbation or during intercourse to help overcome a particular environment or occasion—a time or a place that doesn't turn the individual on.

Masters: Imagination, as we define it, plays a very real part in sexual response, but it varies tremendously with individuals. Usually, it is employed during the excitement or early-plateau phases; but at the moment of orgasmic expression, the individual usually is immersed in his own sensate focus.

Johnson: I do want to emphasize that imagination, as we understand it, relates not to fantasy but to reality, to a recall or use of the realities of a person's life. True fantasy—in other words, the invention of thought patterns related to sex or sexuality—is generally employed by those individuals who have had little or no previous successful experience.

Playboy: Obviously, imagination would have great value with a sex partner who was not physically attractive. Have you found that physical attractiveness is important to successful sex response?

Johnson: Again, all these things are terribly individual. In this society, there are certain stereotypes of attractiveness, but even these have variations. If an individual reminds you of someone else who has brought pleasure, or connotes warmth or other valued attributes, that person is perceived as attractive and thereby sexually stimulating apart from the stereotype. We can't make a general statement except to repeat the perceptive cliché that beauty is in the eye of the beholder.

Playboy: In your experience as investigators, however, aren't there certain aspects of appearance that seem more stimulating than others for many American men—characteristics such as breast size, for example?

Masters: If you talk about breast size, you have to mention Madison Avenue and *Playboy*, because they have created connotations of sexuality in connection with it. As a matter of fact, the larger-breasted female may not be more responsive.

Johnson: Worse yet, a woman's preoccupation with her symbolic sex quality might cancel out her attention to, or her involvement with, her real sexuality. I think that would be the most common pitfall. On the other hand, her symbolic sexual qualities might make her conceive of herself as more of a sexual person; consequently, she might involve herself with more enthusiasm. I'm not an anthropologist, but I think there is evidence that the attraction of the female breast relates to the mother-figure concept.

Masters: And yet, in the male population, there are hip watchers, leg watchers. It varies.

Playboy: Do you have any idea how these individual predilections develop?

Masters: Personal conditioning, I would guess. Maybe the first exposure to sexuality was a woman with particularly attractive legs or breasts.

Playboy: In your experience, are women aroused by the sight of male nudity?

Masters: Kinsey felt that the female was essentially unaroused by the unclothed male, but this has not been the case in our experience.

Johnson: We have come through an era in which the male body was considered quite unbeautiful. Men wore tops at the beaches, and so on. Many women built in a rejection. They weren't supposed to look, but sometimes they did and liked what they saw; so their private and public behavior were quite different. Given equal opportunity, women will react to sexual anatomy just as men do—just as much or just as little, if society permits them to and if they begin to think of themselves as sexual beings.

Playboy: Would you make the same generalization about pornography—that it has equal erotic potential for women and for men?

Masters: According to our experience, yes. The greatest variations relate to an individual's background and personal preference, rather than to his or her sex.

Playboy: Do you think pornography would continue to have its arousing effects if it were made more easily available and lost its taboo quality?

Johnson: Our attitude, like everyone else's, is purely speculative. But we think pornography certainly gains in its excitement by being forbidden.

Playboy: The kind of progress you're talking about is part of what's been called the Sexual Revolution—a revolution that is defined in many ways by many people. Can you give us your own definition?

Johnson: To begin with, we don't call it a revolution; we call it a renaissance. People tend to forget that the greatest deterrent to female freedom of sexual expression in this country was the invention of the steamboat—in other words, the Industrial Revolution.

Masters: It was this that pulled the men off the farms and into the city. In an agricultural community, female sexual equality never became an issue. Time and time again, mom—in order to avoid the kids—would take pop's lunch out into the back field. They had lunch —and something more—by the creek under a shade tree. Fulfillment was thus taken for granted. Sex in this culture was presumed, valued, enjoyed—and lived. Then as we became an industrial culture, puritanism spread and eventually Victorianism took over. With it came the repression of female sexuality that has existed until very recent years—the "thou shalt nots," the double standard, and so on.

Johnson: So you see, we're talking about a *rebirth* of natural sexuality. We're beginning to hark back to a time when there was an earthy acceptance of oneself as a sexual being, when sex was taken for granted as a healthy part of life. If I may inject a personal note, our work is very much a reflection of this renaissance. Even though people have been somewhat shaken by it, society has still *permitted* it.

Masters: Precisely. We have not existed in spite of our time; we have existed *because* of it.

Johnson: Actually, Kinsey was a pioneer—and so were R. L. Dickenson and Havelock Ellis before him. But they reflected a deep cultural need. We have emerged as a reflection of society's changing attitudes. For example, Bill started as a gynecologist—a physician— and I know that his early interest in the basic science of sex research developed almost parallel with the maturation of society's attitudes toward the subject. Kinsey, on the other hand, pioneered this renaissance; he helped lead it and make it what it is.

Playboy: Many critics of this sexual renaissance, as you know, think that the pendulum has swung too far in the direction of permissiveness, that the new emphasis on sex has inflated its importance out of proper proportion. Are we correct in assuming that you disagree?

Masters: If the importance of sex was ever overemphasized—by its obsessive and moralistic negation—it was in the Victorian period, not now. It was then, not now, that sex could not be accepted and that sexuality was denied as a dimension of the total personality. If the pendulum has swung too far, I'm sure it will swing back. Let's put it this way: A certain amount of healthy objectivity needs to be injected into the field. We hope that something like this interview—appearing in the magazine I regard as the best available medium for sex education in America today—will help do it.

Playboy: You are obviously pleased to see the double standard disappear. But many clergymen fear that the vanishing "thou shalt nots" are being replaced by libertarian "thou shalts" that may deprive young women, by virtue of a kind of reverse puritanism, of their freedom of choice. Do you see this happening?

Masters: Absolutely not. What has developed with the use of contraception is a new sense of selectivity for young women. They now have more freedom to say no than they ever had before. It may have something to do with the fact that the female no longer makes her decisions on the basis of fear—fear of pregnancy, fear of disease, fear of social ostracism. In no sense does this imply a rejection of elective chastity, but chastity based on the innumerable fears is entirely a false premise; an objective decision cannot be made on this basis. Today the young woman is free to make her choice, pick her time, her place, her circumstance, without the old fears. With all the druthers now available to her, we have a hunch that the intelligent girl tends to be more sophisticated in her selection—simply because it is *her* selection.

Johnson: If effective contraception is being used, then a woman must be honest with herself and realize that she is engaging in sexual activity as an expression of herself within a relationship. She is not, consciously or unconsciously, playing the old game of sex for marriage entrapment nor is she using sex to represent her femaleness by "willful exposure to unwanted pregnancy"—to quote Dr. Hans Lehfeldt's tongue-in-cheek but accurate comment.

Playboy: Do you think it's possible, as some clergymen predict, that the elimination of fear will break down all the barriers?

Masters: Is it possible? Yes. But there is no reason to believe that removal of fear inevitably results in the destruction of value systems. In fact, there is some evidence that modern young men and women are much more concerned with the quality of interpersonal relationships than with sex per se.

Johnson: What I'm about to say may not go over well with some *Playboy* readers, but the fact is that for the first time in many decades, the girl is running the sexual show. She is not a victim; she doesn't have to put up or shut up. Although this issue is still in limbo, we're on the right road toward placing value on sexual activity within a human relationship as opposed to simple emphasis on natural drives —you know, "Let's do it, even though the timing is wrong, the people are wrong and the place is wrong; we have to satisfy a natural human need." The young woman now has many things to contemplate in making her choice. She can decide, after proper self-evaluation, whether her goal is reproduction and homemaking or whether she wants to express herself in some other fashion while deferring—or even rejecting—marriage. There are so many options to consider, and the concerns of venereal disease, pregnancy or social ostracism need no longer be the foremost factors in influencing her decision.

Epilogue

The selections in this book have dealt with the nature of sex differences in personality and have offered some theories as to their origin and significance. But they have not really addressed themselves to the *meaning* of such differences as they relate to our daily lives. This omission was, to some extent, deliberate, both on the part of the researchers responsible for these studies (since scientists feel obligated to stay out of the arena of value judgments) and on my part (because I share this respect for the objectivity of science). Yet it is difficult, and perhaps deeply unjust, to leave this topic without at least commenting on some of the problems posed by the attempt to place existing sex differences within the framework of contemporary social values.

The recent resurgence of Women's Liberation movements, which form part of a general movement for increased equality for all people in our society, has focused attention on just these value issues. And the problem that Women's Lib poses for both adherents and opponents of its viewpoints, of either sex, is among the most basic dilemmas of our society. The paradox can be stated in its most extreme terms as follows: if you are dedicated to the proposition that all people should be allowed freedom of choice whenever possible, what do you do with an individual who chooses a life of slavery?

This problem has arisen in the most poignant form possible in the black American's recent struggle for equality. Until he started fighting back, most people (himself included) just "knew" that he was more contented being taken care of by "Ol' Massa" on the plantation —that he did not *want* the responsibilities of equal rights. Attitude surveys among blacks clearly showed that, whether or not they really *were* inferior to whites in intelligence, ambition, or any other quality, they actually *felt* they were and in fact were content with inferior roles.

The same arguments can be and, indeed, are applied to male-female relations, particularly by female opponents of Women's Lib. The selections in this book by Goldberg, MacBrayer, and Schaeffer and Eisenberg all provide evidence to indicate that, whether or not women are equal to men in the traits being assessed, they themselves feel that females in general are inferior to males. And if (the argument goes) women are content with their delicate, frilly roles in their gilded cages—*if that is what they really want* (and research indicates that it is)—why not let them have it? It is, after all, a freely selected form of slavery.

But is that enough? Scientists who also have commitments to value systems have argued that it is not and cannot be. If an individual, through the force of his constitutional endowment or social upbringing, honestly feels inferior—honestly chooses slavery—then the goal of science is *not* to solemnly record this fact and allow the bigots to take advantage of it. Rather, the goal of science is to find some way to change that constitutional endowment or that social environment in such a manner as to enable the individual to feel that he is the equal of others. The concerned scientist, aware of his social role, may even feel an ethical obligation to suppress information or knowledge that he has collected, in deliberate violation of one of the first principles of the scientific ethic, if he feels that it can be misused in such a manner.

Similarly, it may be argued that this book should never have been written; I am in almost perfect sympathy with such an argument. The import of Goldberg's data, and those of my own study, leaves me deeply appalled at what society has done to the self-image of half its members. I find the protestations of many feminine opponents of Women's Lib almost as moving as the withdrawal symptoms of a drug addict. But I cannot, for that reason or any other, believe that the matter would be improved by the suppression of this information. Although I cannot begin to offer solutions to the problems created by the unequal treatment and expectations accorded the sexes from birth or by their immediate and extended society, I also cannot feel that we will draw any nearer to a solution if we pretend these problems don't exist. However, we will, if we pretend they don't exist, offer less fuel for the bigots.

But before turning the field over entirely to the forces of bigotry, let's try to see what alternatives science may suggest. I've offered, in this book, examples of two more or less competing theories of the origins of sex differences in personality: the Freudian and the social learning. It is to such theories that we must look if we are interested in changing the present pattern of personality differences. The Freudian theory argues, in essence, that it is the child's early awareness of the constitutional, physiological differences between the sexes that affects his relationship with his parents in such a manner as to bring about the distinctive psychological differences. This changed relationship, moreover, is characterized primarily by the development of the strong, punitive superego in the male and the weaker, retaliatory superego in the female. The social learning position argues instead that it is the direct social interaction between parents and child, unmediated by any special perception of physiological differences, that leads to the adult psychological differences. A critical element for this position is the father's relative absence from the home, which results in the lack of a direct model for masculine behaviors. Clearly the two theories are not very far apart. Less clearly they both appear to be a little outdated.

Consider the question of how to effect changes in the adult psyche so that both sexes see themselves as equal. According to Freudian viewpoints, it would appear that this could be done either by strengthening the superego of the female child or by weakening that of the male. The former course is difficult: the development of the superego hinges on the perception of the penis, which the girl lacks. Moreover, the idea is slightly repellent to contemporary value systems, which tend to encourage looseness and self-expression rather than rigidity and control. Is there any way, then, of weakening the male superego —other than castrating him at an early age? Obviously there is. The boy will not fear castration unless he views his father as threatening and his mother as both attractive and unattainable. If this view can be changed, the massive repression of sexual impulses out of which the superego grows would not occur and the male would not see himself as superior to the female.

Now consider the same question with regard to the social learning position. There the matter seems even simpler: put the father back in the home, or take the mother out, and the selective, differential modeling opportunities would no longer be present and later sex differences would be far less pronounced.

But all these changes have been occurring in our society over the last two or three decades. Fathers, aware of Freud and of their emotional responsibilities to children, seem to have become much less threatening and authoritarian and much more permissive; mothers have become much less unattainable and much more encouraging of emotional interactions with their children. At the same time, many mothers have turned to vocations outside of the home and fathers have begun to share in the diapers-and-discipline routines. It would seem that today's society is drawing closer to those conditions necessary for sexual equality all by itself, without any real prodding by value-oriented scientists.

Striking evidence for this position is found in a recent study by

Whittaker (1969), who investigated a sample of today's more emancipated or liberal adolescents: the Berkeley "underground" or "nonstudent" group. Using more than 150 volunteer subjects, each of whom took a battery of psychological tests, Whittaker found that the traditional sex norms associated with these tests virtually disappeared in his subjects. The males were markedly more "feminine" in their values, interests, and introspections than either their college-student counterparts or the published norms for the tests; the females were, to a lesser extent, more "masculine" in these areas than their counterparts. As a result, the precautionary preanalysis breaking of data into different samples for males and females, which is virtually taken for granted in most studies of personality, turned out to be unnecessary for this group.

Whittaker's interpretation of these findings is cautious. He suggests that his subjects may be more neurotic, marginal, or misplaced than normal college students. But, on the other hand, they may merely be open to more and different experiences and less defensive and stereotyped in their attitudes than their "normal" counterparts.

I prefer the latter explanation. I find support for it in the gradual warming and easing of family relationships in our society in recent years. I find further support for it in the very existence of Women's Liberation activities, which themselves indicate that women now feel nearly enough equal to men to ask for full equality. And I am hopeful that society, as it muddles along the incredibly difficult road to justice and equality for all, will manage to avail itself of the opportunities that even a science blind to values offers it—refinements in technology that ease the housewife out of her trap or refinements in our knowledge of ourselves and others that allow most of us to live now with the awareness that we are far from perfect but nevertheless worthwhile. If society can do this (and Whittaker's study suggests it is), my book may speedily become obsolete—which would be the sincerest form of flattery.

References

Abraham, K. Manifestations of the female castration complex (1921). *Selected papers.* London: Hogarth, 1927.

Adams, E.B., & Sarason, I.G. Relation between anxiety in children and their parents. *Child Development,* 1963, **34,** 237-246.

Adorno, T., Frenkel-Brunswik, E., Levinson, D., & Sanford, R. *The authoritarian personality.* New York: Harper, 1950.

Aldous, J., & Kell, L. A partial test of some theories of identification. *Journal of Marriage and Family Living,* 1961, **23,** 15-19.

Allen, V.L., & Crutchfield, R.S. Generalization of experimentally reinforced conformity. *Journal of Abnormal and Social Psychology,* 1963, **67,** 326-333.

Allport, G.W. *The nature of prejudice.* Reading, Mass.: Addison-Wesley, 1954.

Anastasi, A. *Differential psychology.* New York: Macmillan, 1966.

Ardrey, R. *The territorial imperative.* New York: Atheneum, 1966.

Bayley, N. Size and body build of adolescents in relation to role of skeletal maturing. *Child Development,* 1943, **14,** 51-89.

Bennett, E.M., & Cohen, L.R. Men and women, personality patterns and contrasts. *Genetic Psychology Monographs,* 1959, **59,** 101-155.

Bixenstine, V., Chambers, N., & Wilson, K.V. Effect of asymmetry in payoff on behavior in a two-person non-zero-sum game. *Journal of Conflict Resolution,* 1963, **8,** 151-159.

Bixenstine, V., & Wilson, K.V. Effects of level of cooperative choice by the other player on choices in the Prisoner's Dilemma game. *Journal of Abnormal and Social Psychology,* 1963, **67,** 139-147.

Blanchard, P. A study of the subject matter and motivation of children's dreams. *Journal of Abnormal and Social Psychology,* 1926, **21,** 24-37.

Blum, G.S. A reply to Steward's "Psychoanalysis, deductive methods, and the Blacky Test." *Journal of Abnormal and Social Psychology,* 1950, **45,** 536-537.

Blum, G.S. *Psychoanalytic theories of personality.* New York: McGraw-Hill, 1953.

Blum, G.S. *Model of the mind.* New York: Wiley, 1961.

Bond, J.R., & Vinacke, W.E. Coalitions in mixed-sex triads. *Sociometry,* 1961, **24,** 71-75.

Brown, D.G. Sex-role development in a changing culture. *Psychological Bulletin,* 1958, **55,** 232-242.

Brown, N.O. *Life against death.* Middletown, Conn.: Wesleyan University Press, 1959.

Bruner, J.S., & Goodman, C.C. Value and need as organizing factors in perception. *Journal of Abnormal and Social Psychology,* 1947, **42,** 33-44.

Brunswik, E. *The conceptual framework of psychology.* Chicago: University of Chicago Press, 1952.

Brunswik, E. *Perception and the representative design of experiments.* Berkeley: University of California Press, 1956.

Burgess, E.W., & Wallin, P. *Engagement and marriage.* Philadelphia: Lippincott, 1953.

Buss, A. *The psychology of aggression.* New York: Wiley, 1961.

Byrne, D. Response to humor as a function of drive arousal and psychological defense. Unpublished doctoral dissertation, Stanford University, 1957.

Carlson, J.S., Cook, S.W., & Stromberg, E.L. Sex differences in conversation. *Journal of Applied Psychology*, 1936, **20,** 727-735.

Carmichael, L. (Ed.) *Manual of child psychology.* New York: Wiley, 1954.

Carter, L.F., & Schooler, K. Value, need, and other factors in perception. *Psychological Review*, 1949, **56,** 200-207.

Centers, R. *The psychology of social classes.* Princeton, N.J.: Princeton University Press, 1949.

Coles, R. *Children of crisis: A study of courage and fear.* New York: Atlantic-Little, Brown, 1967.

Crafts, L.F., Schneirla, T.C., Robinson, E.E., & Gilbert, R.W. *Recent experiments in psychology.* New York: McGraw-Hill, 1950.

Deutsch, H. *Zur Psychologie der weiblichen Sexualfunktionen* (On female sexuality). Vienna: Internationaler Psychoanalytischer Verlag, 1925.

Doris, J., & Fierman, E. Humor and anxiety. *Journal of Abnormal and Social Psychology*, 1956, **53,** 59-62.

Emmerich, W. Young children's discrimination of parent and child roles. *Child Development*, 1959, **30,** 403-419.

Everett, E.G. Behavioral characteristics of early- and late-maturing girls. Unpublished master's thesis, University of California, 1943.

Fenichel, O. *The psychoanalytic theory of neurosis.* New York: Norton, 1945.

Fernberger, S.W. Persistence of stereotypes concerning sex differences. *Journal of Abnormal and Social Psychology*, 1948, **43,** 97-101.

Festinger, L. *A theory of cognitive dissonance.* Evanston, Ill.: Row and Peterson, 1957.

Fiedler, L. *Love and death in the American novel.* New York: Criterion, 1960.

Fisher, R.A. *Statistical methods for research workers* (7th ed.) Edinburgh: Oliver and Boyd, 1938.

Franck, K. Preference for sex symbols and their personality correlation. *Genetic Psychology Monographs*, 1946, **33** (2).

French, E., & Lesser, G.S. Some characteristics of the achievement motive in women. *Journal of Abnormal and Social Psychology*, 1964, **68,** 119-128.

Freud, S. *Interpretation of dreams* (1900), Standard Edition, Vols. 4-5. London: Hogarth, 1924.

Freud, S. *On dreams* (1901). New York: Norton, 1952.

Freud, S. *Three essays on the theory of sexuality* (1905a), Standard Edition, Vol. 7. London: Hogarth, 1924.

Freud, S. Fragment of an analysis of a case of hysteria (1905b). *Collected papers*, Vol. 3. London: Hogarth, 1925.

Freud, S. On the sexual theories of children (1908). *Collected papers*, Vol. 2. London: Hogarth, 1924.

Freud, S. On narcissism (1914a). *Collected papers*, Vol. 4. London: Hogarth, 1924.

Freud, S. On the history of the psychoanalytic movement (1914b). *Collected papers*, Vol. 1. London: Hogarth, 1924.

Freud, S. *Introductory lectures on psychoanalysis.* London: Allen and Unwin, 1922.

Freud, S. The passing of the Oedipus complex (1924). *Collected papers*, Vol. 2. London: Hogarth, 1924.

Freud, S. Some psychological consequences of the anatomical distinction between the sexes (1925). *Collected papers*, Vol. 5. London: Hogarth, 1952.

Freud, S. Female sexuality (1931). *Collected papers*, Vol. 5. London: Hogarth, 1952.

Freud, S. *New introductory lectures on psychoanalysis* (1933). New York: Norton, 1933.

Freud, S. Wit and its relation to the unconscious. In A.A. Brill (Ed.), *The basic writings of Sigmund Freud*. New York: Random House, 1938.

Goldberg, L.R. The proliferation of personality scales and inventories: An historical analysis. In P. MacReynolds (Ed.), *Advances in psychological assessment*, Vol. 2. Palo Alto, Calif.: Science and Behavior Books, 1970.

Goldberg, P. Are women prejudiced against women? *Trans-action*, 1968, **5**, 28-30.

Goodenough, E.W. Interest in persons as an aspect of sex difference in the early years. *Genetic Psychology Monographs*, 1957, **55**, 287-323.

Goodfield, B.A. A preliminary paper on the development of the time intensity compensation hypothesis in masculine identification. Paper read at San Francisco State Psychological Convention, April 1965.

Gordon, H. A comparative study of dreams and responses to the Thematic Apperception Test: A need-press analysis. *Journal of Personality*, 1954, **22**, 234-253.

Gray, S.W., & Klaus, R. The assessment of parental identification. *Genetic Psychology Monographs*, 1956, **54**, 87-114.

Greenstein, F.I. Sex-related political differences in childhood. *Journal of Politics*, 1961, **23**, 353-371.

Guetzkow, H. An analysis of the operation of set in problem-solving behavior. *Journal of Genetic Psychology*, 1951, **45**, 219-244.

Hall, C.S. Diagnosing personality by the analysis of dreams. *Journal of Abnormal and Social Psychology*, 1947, **42**, 68-79.

Hall, C.S. *Manual for dream analysis*. Department of Psychology, Western Reserve University, 1949. (Mimeo.)

Hall, C.S. A cognitive theory of dream symbols. *Journal of General Psychology*, 1953, **48**, 169-186.

Hall, C.S. Strangers in dreams: An empirical confirmation of the Oedipal complex. *Journal of Personality*, 1963, **31**, 336-345.

Hall, C.S., & Domhoff, B. A ubiquitous sex difference in dreams. *Journal of Abnormal and Social Psychology*, 1963, **66**, 278-280.

Hall, C.S., & Van de Castle, R.L. An empirical investigation of the castration complex in dreams. *Journal of Personality*, 1965, **33**, 20-29.

Hammond, K.R. New directions in research on conflict resolution. *Journal of Social Issues*, 1965, **21**, 44-66.

Hammond, K.R. Cognition and conflict. Unpublished manuscript, Institute for Behavioral Sciences, University of Colorado. Report #100, 1967.

Hammond, K.R. Inductive knowing. Paper presented at the Second Conference for Theoretical Psychology, Banff, Alberta, Canada, 1969.

Hammond, K.R., Bartoli-Bonaituo, G., Faucheux, C., Moscovici, S., Frohlich, W., Joyce, C.R.B., & di Majo, G. Cognitive conflict between persons in Western Europe and the United States: A comparison. *Journal of International Psychology*, 1968, **3**, 1-11.

Hammond, K.R., & Brehmer, B. *Distrust among nations: A challenge to scientific inquiry*. Boulder, Colo.: Institute of Behavioral Sciences, Report #116, 1969.

Hammond, K.R., Todd, F.J., Wilkins, M., & Mitchell, T.O. Cognitive conflict between persons: Applications of the "lens model" paradigm. *Journal of Experimental and Social Psychology*, 1966, **2**, 234-260.

Harrison, R. The Thematic Apperception Test. In L.K. Frank et al., Personality development in adolescent girls. *Monographs of the Society for Research in Child Development*, 1951, **16**, 60-88.

Hartley, R.E. Sex-role pressures and the socialization of the male child. *Psychological Reports*, 1959, **5**, 458.

Hattwick, L.A. Sex differences in the behavior of nursery school children. *Child Development*, 1937, **8**, 343-355.

Hilgard, E.R. *Introduction to psychology*. New York: Harcourt, 1962.

Holt, R.R. Beyond vitalism and mechanism: Freud's concept of psychic energy. In B. Wolman (Ed.), *Historical roots of contemporary psychology*. New York: Harper, 1966.

Honzik, P. Sex differences in the occurrence of materials in the play constructions of pre-adolescents. *Child Development*, 1951, **22**, 15-35.

Horney, K. On the genesis of the castration complex in women. *International Journal of Psychoanalysis*, 1923, **5**, 50-65.

Hunt, T. The measurement of social intelligence. *Journal of Applied Psychology*, 1928, **12**, 317-333.

Husband, R.W. Sex differences in dream content. *Journal of Abnormal and Social Psychology*, 1936, **30**, 513-521.

Institute of Dream Research. *A manual for classifying aggressions, misfortunes, friendly acts and good fortune in dreams*. Miami, Fla.: Author, 1962.

Jackson, V.D. The measurement of social proficiency. *Journal of Experimental Education*, 1940, **8**, 422-474.

Jones, H.E. Observational methods in the study of individual development. *Journal of Consulting Psychology*, 1940, **4**, 234-238.

Jones, H.E. *Development in adolescence*. New York: Appleton, 1943.

Jones, H.E. Adolescence in our society. In *The family in a democratic society: Anniversary papers of the Community Service Society of New York*. New York: Columbia University Press, 1949.

Jones, M.C. A study of socialization at the high school level. *Journal of Genetic Psychology*, 1958, **93**, 87-111.

Jones, M.C., & Bayley, N. Physical maturing among boys as related to behavior. *Journal of Educational Psychology*, 1950, **41**, 129-148.

Kagan, J., Hosken, B., & Watson, S. The child's symbolic conceptualization of the parents. *Child Development*, 1961, **32**, 625-636.

Kagan, J., & Lemkin, J. The child's differential perception of parental attributes. *Journal of Abnormal and Social Psychology*, 1960, **61**, 446-447.

Kephart, W.M. *The family, society and the individual*. Boston: Houghton Mifflin, 1961.

Kimmins, C.W. *Children's dreams*. New York: Longmans-Green, 1920.

King, J.E. *Factored aptitude series*. Chicago: Industrial Psychology, 1947.

Kinsey, A.C., Pomeroy, W.B., & Martin, C.E. *Sexual behavior in the human male*. Philadelphia: Saunders, 1948.

Kinsey, A. C., Pomeroy, W. B., Martin, C. E., & Gebhard, P. H. *Sexual behavior in the human female*. Philadelphia: Saunders, 1953.

Kitay, P.M. A comparison of the sexes in their attitudes and beliefs about women: A study of prestige groups. *Sociometry*, 1940, **3**, 399-407.

Kohlberg, L. Cognitive-developmental analysis of children's sex-role concepts and attitudes. In E.E. Maccoby (Ed.), *Development of sex differences*. Stanford, Calif.: Stanford University Press, 1966.

Komorita, S.S. Cooperative choice in a Prisoner's Dilemma game. *Journal of Personality and Social Psychology*, 1965, **2**, 741-745.

Kostich, M.M. A study of transfer: Sex differences in the reasoning process. *Journal of Personality*, 1954, **45**, 449-458.

Landis, C. National differences in conversations. *Journal of Abnormal and Social Psychology*, 1927, **21**, 354-357.

Landis, M.M., & Burtt, M.E. A study of conversations. *Journal of Comparative Psychology*, 1924, **4**, 81-89.

Lazowick, L.M. On the nature of identification. *Journal of Abnormal and Social Psychology*, 1955, **51**, 175-183.

Lorenz, K. *On aggression* (1963). New York: Harcourt, 1966.

Luchins, A.S., & Luchins, E.H. *Rigidity of behavior*. Eugene: University of Oregon Press, 1959.

Lynn, D.B. A note on sex differences in the development of masculine and feminine identification. *Psychological Review*, 1959, **66**, 126-135.

Lynn, D.B. Sex differences in identification development. *Sociometry*, 1961, **24**, 372-383.

Lynn, D.B. Sex-role and parental identification. *Child Development*, 1962, **33**, 555-564.

Lynn, D.B. Divergent feedback and sex-role identification in boys and men. *Merrill-Palmer Quarterly*, 1964, **10**, 17-23.

MacBrayer, C.T. Differences in perception of the opposite sex by males and females. *Journal of Social Psychology*, 1960, **52**, 309-314.

Maccoby, E. E. (Ed.) *Development of sex differences*. Stanford, Calif.: Stanford University Press, 1966.

Marcuse, H. *Eros and civilization*. Boston: Beacon, 1955.

Masters, W.H., & Johnson, V.E. *Human sexual response*. Boston: Little, Brown, 1966.

Masters, W.H., & Johnson, V. E. *Human sexual inadequacy*. Boston: Little, Brown, 1970.

McClelland, D.C. On the psychodynamics of creative physical scientists. In H.E. Gruber, G. Terrell, & M. Wertheimer (Eds.), *Contemporary approaches to creative thinking*. New York: Atherton, 1964.

McKee, J.P., & Sherriffs, A.C. The differential evaluation of males and females. *Journal of Personality*, 1957, **25**, 356-371.

Mead, M. *Male and female*. New York: Morrow, 1949.

Meer, S.J. Authoritarian attitudes and dreams. *Journal of Abnormal and Social Psychology*, 1955, **51**, 74-78.

Moore, H.T. Further data concerning sex differences. *Journal of Abnormal and Social Psychology*, 1922, **17**, 210-214.

Moss, F.A. Do you know how to get along with people? Why some people get ahead in the world while others do not. *Scientific American*, 1926, **135**, 26-27.

Moss, F.A., & Hunt, T. Are you socially intelligent? An analysis of the scores of 7000 persons on the George Washington University Social Intelligence Test. *Scientific American*, 1927, **137**, 108-110.

Moss, F. A., Hunt, T., & Omwake, K. T. *Social intelligence test* (rev. form, 1st ed.) Washington, D. C.: George Washington University, 1930.

Moss, F.A., Hunt, T., Omwake, K.T., & Woodward, L.G. *Social intelligence test* (rev. form, 2nd ed.) Washington, D.C.: George Washington University, 1949.

Mussen, P.H., & Jones, M.C. Self-conceptions, motivations, and interpersonal attitudes of late- and early-maturing boys. *Child Development*, 1957, **28**, 243-256.

Mussen, P.H., & Naylor, H.K. The relationship between overt and fantasy aggression. *Journal of Abnormal and Social Psychology*, 1954, **49**, 235-240.

Nakamura, C.F. Conformity and problem solving. *Journal of Abnormal and Social Psychology*, 1958, **56**, 315-320.

Newman, F.B. The adolescent in social groups. *Applied Psychology Monographs*, 1946, **9**.

Oetzel, R. Annotated bibliography. In E.E. Maccoby (Ed.), *The development of sex differences*. Stanford, Calif.: Stanford University Press, 1966.

Parsons, T. The social structure of the family. In R. Anshen (Ed.), *The family: Its function and destiny*. New York: Harper, 1959.

Polster, E. An investigation of ego-functioning in dreams. Unpublished doctoral dissertation, Western Reserve University, 1950.

Pope, H.L. Prohibitions, self-deceptions, and dreams. Unpublished doctoral dissertation, Western Reserve University, 1952.

Rapaport, D. The structure of psychoanalytic theory: A systematizing attempt. In S. Koch (Ed.), *Psychology: A study of a science*, Vol. 3. New York: McGraw-Hill, 1959.

Rapaport, D., & Gill, M.M. The points of view and assumptions of metapsychology. *International Journal of Psychoanalysis*, 1959, **40**, 153-162.

Rappoport, A., & Chammah, A. Sex differences in factors contributing to the level of cooperation in the Prisoner's Dilemma game. *Journal of Personality and Social Psychology*, 1965, **2**, 831-838.

Riesman, D. *The lonely crowd*. New Haven, Conn.: Yale University Press, 1950.

Sacks, J. M., & Levy, S. The sentence completion test. In L. E. Abt & L. Bellak (Eds.), *Projective psychology*. New York: Knopf, 1952.

Sarason, S. Dreams and Thematic Apperception Test stories. *Journal of Abnormal and Social Psychology*, 1944, **39**, 486-492.

Scheinfeld, A. *Women and men*. New York: Harcourt, 1943.

Seward, J. P. Psychoanalysis, deductive methods, and the Blacky Test. *Journal of Abnormal and Social Psychology*, 1950, **45**, 529-535.

Sherriffs, A.C., & Jarrett, R.F. Sex differences in attitudes about sex differences. *Journal of Psychology*, 1953, **35**, 161-168.

Shuttleworth, F.K. Sexual maturation and the physical growth of girls age 6 to 19. *Monographs of the Society for Research in Child Development*, 1937, **2**.

Shuttleworth, F.K. The physical and mental growth of girls and boys age 6 to 19 in relation to age at maximum growth. *Monographs of the Society for Research in Child Development*, 1939, **4**.

Smith, S. Age and sex differences in children's opinions concerning sex differences. *Journal of Genetic Psychology*, 1939, **54**, 17-25.

Snedecor, W.W. *Statistical methods*. Ames: Iowa State College Press, 1946.

Spiegel, D. *The Spiegel Personality Inventory: Test booklet and manual*. Los Angeles: Author, 1965.

Spiegel, D., Olivo, M., & Keith-Spiegel, P. Tactual appeal and aversion: Validation of three predictors. *Journal of Projective Techniques and Personality Assessment*, 1968, **32**, 82-87.

Stolz, H.R., & Stolz, L.M. Adolescent problems related to somatic variations. *Yearbook of the National Society for the Study of Education*, 1944, **43**, 80-99.

Strickland, J. The effect of motivation on human preferences. *Journal of Abnormal and Social Psychology*, 1959. **59**, 278-281.

Strong, E.K., Jr. *Vocational interests of men and women*. Stanford, Calif.: Stanford University Press, 1943.

Taylor, J. A personality scale of manifest anxiety. *Journal of Abnormal and Social Psychology*, 1953, **48**, 285-290.

Terman, L.M. Kinsey's "Sexual Behavior in the Human Male": Some comments and criticisms. *Psychological Bulletin*, 1948, **45**, 443-459.

Terman, L.M., & Miles, C.C. *Sex and personality: Studies in masculinity and femininity.* New York: McGraw-Hill, 1936.

Thorndike, R.L. Factor analysis of social and abstract intelligence. *Journal of Educational Psychology*, 1936, **27**, 231-233.

Thorndike, R.L., & Stein, S. An evaluation of attempts to measure social intelligence. *Psychological Bulletin*, 1937, **34**, 275-285.

Tolman, E.C. *Purposive behavior in animals and men.* New York: Century, 1932.

Tryon, C.M. Evaluations of adolescent personality by adolescents. *Monographs of the Society for Research in Child Development*, 1939a, **4**.

Tryon, C.M. *U.C. Adjustment Inventory I: Social and emotional adjustment.* Berkeley: University of California Press, 1939b.

Tuddenham, R.D. Studies in reputation: III. Correlates of popularity among elementary school children. *Journal of Educational Psychology*, 1951, **42**, 257-276.

Tuddenham, R.D. Studies in reputation: I. Sex and grade differences in school children's evaluation of their peers. *Psychology Monographs*, 1952, **66** (1).

Tyler, L.E. *Psychology of human differences.* New York: Appleton, 1965.

Uesugi, T. K., & Vinacke, W. E. Strategy in a feminine game. *Sociometry*, 1963, **26**, 75-88.

Vinacke, N.E. Sex roles in a three person game. *Sociometry*, 1959, **22**, 343-359.

Waelder, R. *Basic theory of psychoanalysis.* New York: International Universities Press, 1960.

Wallach, M.A., & Caron, A.J. Attribute criteriality and sex-linked conservatism as determinants of psychological similarity. *Journal of Abnormal and Social Psychology*, 1959, **59**, 43-50.

Wallach, M.A., & Kagan, N. Sex differences and judgment process. *Journal of Personality*, 1959, **27**, 555-564.

Watson, J., Breed, W., & Posman, M. A study in urban conversation: A sample of 1001 remarks overheard in Manhattan. *Journal of Social Psychology*, 1948, **28**, 121-123.

Whittaker, D. Masculinity-femininity and nonconformist youth. *Proceedings of the 77th Annual Convention of the American Psychological Association*, 1969, pp. 297-298.

Wiggins, N., & Wiggins, J.S. A typological analysis of male preferences for female body types. *Multivariate Behavioral Research*, 1969, **4**, 89-102.

Wiggins, J. S., Wiggins, N., & Conger, J. C. Correlates of heterosexual somatic preference. *Journal of Personality and Social Psychology*, 1968, **10**, 82-90.

Witkin, M.A., Dyk, R.B., Faterson, H.F., Goodenough, D.R., & Karp, S.A. *Psychological differentiation.* New York: Wiley, 1962.

Woodrow, H. The common factors in fifty-two mental tests. *Psychometrika*, 1939, **4**, 99-108.

Woodworth, R.S., & Schlosberg, H. *Experimental psychology.* New York: Holt, 1954.

Zachry, C.B. *Emotion and conduct in adolescence.* New York: Appleton, 1940.

Zilboorg, G. Masculine and feminine: Some biological and cultural aspects. *Psychiatry*, 1944, **7**, 257-296.

Index